DERBY FEVER

Jim Bolus

PELICAN PUBLISHING COMPANY
Gretna 1995

Library of Congress Cataloging-in-Publication Data

Bolus, Jim.
Derby fever / Jim Bolus.
p. cm.
ISBN 1-56554-124-3 (hc)
1. Kentucky Derby, Louisville, Ky.—Anecdotes. I. Title.
SF357.K4B62 1995
798.4'009769'44—dc20 94-41492
CIP

Manufactured in the United States of America

Published by Pelican Publishing Company, Inc.
1101 Monroe Street, Gretna, Louisiana 70053

To my family—
Suzanne, Jennifer, Bo, and Tana

Contents

Acknowledgments

Just as I did with *Kentucky Derby Stories* and *Remembering the Derby,* I first wish to acknowledge my indebtedness to Judy Bortner, director of retail operations for the Kentucky Derby Museum. Without her suggesting my name to Pelican Publishing Company, none of the recent books that I have written—*Kentucky Derby Stories, Remembering the Derby,* and *Derby Fever*—would have ever gotten off and running.

Special thanks also goes to head librarian Doris Waren and associate librarian Cathy Schenck at the Keeneland Library. They have always been my right hand in researching horse racing.

I also thank the entire staffs at Churchill Downs and the Kentucky Derby Museum. Thanks, too, to Peggy Lacy Moore and Penny Dailey at the Kentucky Racing Commission and to the Louisville Free Public Library, the New Zealand Thoroughbred Breeders' Association, the New Zealand Racing Conference, *The Blood-Horse,* and the New York Racing Association press office.

Books that have served as research sources include *Run for the Roses, The Kentucky Derby Diamond Jubilee, Down the Stretch, The Great Ones,* and various issues of *The American Racing Manual.*

Many publications have been used through the years in researching chapters that appear in this book, including *The Courier-Journal, The Blood-Horse* magazine, *Lexington Herald-*

Leader, The New York Times, the *1986 Kentucky Derby Souvenir Magazine,* the *1993 Kentucky Derby Official Souvenir Magazine,* the *1994 Kentucky Derby Official Souvenir Magazine, Thoroughbred Times, Inside Source, Daily Racing Form, Spur Magazine,* and *Sports Illustrated,* as well as such now-defunct publications as the *Kentucky Irish American, Turf and Sport Digest,* the *Washington Star,* and *Collier's.*

For photographs, I wish to thank Churchill Downs Inc./Kinetic Corp., Amy Petit at the Keeneland Association, Clay Campbell at the Kentucky Derby Festival, Steve Brown at the New York Racing Association, Jack Guthrie, Rose Blevins, *The Courier-Journal,* Zeljko Cvijanovic, the late Jim Raftery, and my favorite photographer, longtime friend Dick Martin.

Hundreds of people have assisted me and been patient with me over the years, and there isn't enough space to list them all. I would be remiss in not mentioning Jack Price, Dan Quayle, Eddie Sweat, Jack Guthrie, Jeff Davidson, Tom O'Hearn, Seth Hancock, John Sosby, Pat Francis, Henry Wolf, Bridget Sherrill, Herb Stevens, Patrick Hogan, Robert Dawe, Tim Greene, Andrew Stewart, Margaret Fife, Renate Reid, Dennis Diaz, Cam Gambolati, Charles Milbank, Cliff Guilliams, Jack Wilson, Jerry Forke, George Koper, D. Wayne Lukas, Randy Moss, Mark Allen, Jack Weipert, J. Simpson Dean, Sharon Bidwell, and Ina Duncan.

And, finally, I wish to give a *very* special thanks to Suzanne, my best friend, my adviser, my typist, my proofreader . . . and my wife of thirty years.

Introduction

Derby fever—if you've never had a case of it, you don't know what you've missed. Medical science has been unable to find a cure for this malady, which surfaces each spring as the Kentucky Derby draws nearer. Derby fever can strike anybody—owner, trainer, jockey, fan.

I always begin to come down with the early symptoms at Keeneland Race Course in the spring of the year. With the good three-year-olds training and racing at Keeneland in preparation for the Kentucky Derby, I can't help myself. The excitement in the air, the anticipation of the first Saturday in May at Churchill Downs, the "Derby talk" that is ever present at every barn, every bar, and every party, well, it's simply too much for me. I catch Derby fever.

Derby fever can cause people—most notably, owners of three-year-olds—to do strange things. Some of these owners all too often let Derby fever cloud their judgment, and they wind up insisting on running their horses for the roses when these noble steeds would be much better off staying in the barn.

Derby fever is highly contagious, transmitted to even the casual racing fan. At this time of the year, many people who pay little, if any, attention to racing the rest of the year suddenly become interested in this happening that takes place at historic Churchill Downs. Office betting pools throughout the country are a big part of Derby tradition. Somebody (probably not Shakespeare) once put it this way:

> Breathes there a man with soul so dead
> Whose memorandum to his office force said,
> "No Derby pool this year, please"?

This book, which is entitled *Derby Fever,* is another collection of my favorite stories on this grand old race. The chapters cover a wide range of topics—from "the Duke" at the Derby; to the famous Derby photograph of the Fighting Finish in 1933; to my favorite Derby, the 1969 running.

But the chapter that is the longest in this book deals not with a winner or a famous horse. Chances are that you've never even heard of a horse named Holy Land. I picked him to win the 1970 Kentucky Derby, and, to my dismay, he stumbled and fell, losing his jockey. I took a lot of kidding about picking that horse, and I've laughed about it through the years, but in my own mind I've always thought that Holy Land would have finished first or second in that race. If only there was some way to go back and rerun that Derby and arrange for Holy Land to have a clear trip as the big field turned for home. I'd love to know what would have happened in the homestretch. Would he have charged down the stretch and overtaken Dust Commander to win the ninety-sixth Derby? We'll never know.

As I mentioned, people have poked fun at me for picking Holy Land. Most of that kidding took place back in the early 1970s. Now, a quarter of a century later, I thought it was safe to go back out in public without anybody mentioning Holy Land's name, but I was wrong. It so happened that while I was putting the finishing touches on the Holy Land chapter for this book, my wife, Suzanne, and I were invited to have dinner one evening at the home of Dickie Martin and his wife, Kathy. For some unknown reason, Kathy brought up the subject of Holy Land. I wasn't taking notes at the time, but I do remember that she asked me a question that I have heard all too many times: "Whatever happened to Holy

Rustic Claiborne Farm, the home of champions. (Photos by Jim Bolus)

Land?" I think Kathy said something about Holy Land running the wrong way around the track (which didn't happen). I believe she suggested that it wasn't until a later race on the card that Holy Land finally finished the Derby. (That didn't happen either.) It seems to me that she even asked if Holy Land was related to Holy Bull. (The answer is no.)

But, alas, I have the final word on Holy Land. Or words, that is. I have put together many words in the chapter on him. Just call it Holy Land's revenge.

Other chapters are included on such champions as Carry Back, Whirlaway, Exterminator, Secretariat, Spend a Buck, and Nashua. I saw Carry Back win his Derby in 1961 and have become good friends with Jack Price, his trainer and breeder. The Carry Back story is one of my all-time favorites.

Secretariat's Derby in 1973 was a memorable race. He ran a brilliant Derby, setting a track record of 1:59⅖ for the mile and one-quarter. I have now attended thirty-five runnings of the Derby, twenty-one of them since Secretariat. I sometimes wonder how many more Derbies will be run before Secetariat's track record will be broken.

Eddie Sweat, the groom for Secretariat, knew this Triple Crown winner better than anybody, and it was a delight for me to interview him at Churchill Downs for the chapter in this book.

Nashua is one of the greatest horses ever to run in the Derby and lose. He was beaten by a great horse, Swaps, in 1955.

I never had the privilege of meeting John Wayne, but in researching the chapter on "the Duke" at the Derby and talking with people who came in touch with him when he was grand marshal at the 1976 Pegasus Parade, I felt as if I had learned a lot about this folk hero.

I have devoted a chapter to the Stevens family, whose horse-racing roots trace back more than 120 years. I've always said that if I ever owned racehorses, I'd like for Herb Stevens to be my trainer. They don't come any better than this knowledgeable Kentucky hardboot.

Another chapter covers Derby chart callers, those men through the years who have documented the race for posterity.

And then I have written a chapter on the Fighting Finish photograph taken by Wallace Lowry. If Hollywood ever decided to make a movie on a Kentucky Derby, the 1933 running would provide terrific drama. I was fortunate enough to get to know Don Meade, the jockey on the victorious Brokers Tip, and Herb Fisher, who rode second-place Head Play. Of all the interviews I've ever had with Derby participants, the ones I had with Meade and Fisher are among those that I cherish the most.

Through the years, I've conducted hundreds of interviews and written thousands of words about the Derby. I now realize that recording the Derby's history is a never-ending project. The more I learn about the Derby, the more I realize how much more there is to learn.

I hope the chapters in this book provide some inkling as to what this great race is all about . . . this race that causes so many of us to get Derby fever every spring.

DERBY FEVER

"Thunder Over Louisville" fireworks show at the Derby Festival opening ceremonies. (Photo by Jonathan Roberts, courtesy Derby Festival)

1

The Kentucky Derby: Truly a Happening

THE KENTUCKY DERBY IS HAILED as "the greatest two minutes in sports," but it's so much more than just a horse race. It's a social affair, with high society entertaining guests at lavish parties. It's a vacation for thousands of collegians who converge on the Churchill Downs infield for a day of fun and frolic and who knows what else. And it's an afternoon when the rich and the famous *want to be seen.*

The Derby also is a civic celebration, one that turns Louisville upside down and inside out, affecting the community to such an extent that a long extravaganza—the Kentucky Derby Festival—is held to celebrate the event. A whirlwind of more than seventy events, the festival ran for seventeen days in 1994, boasting such major attractions as "Thunder Over Louisville," heralded as North America's largest fireworks show and drawing more spectators—perhaps even many more—than the Derby, the miniMarathon, the Great Balloon Race, the Pegasus Parade, and the Great Steamboat Race, which for most of its history has matched the *Delta Queen* and the *Belle of Louisville.*

The Kentucky Derby is all these things—a social occasion,

The Great Balloon Race. (Photo by Daniel Dempster, courtesy Derby Festival)

The Great Steamboat Race. (Photo by Richard Bram, courtesy Derby Festival)

The Pegasus Parade. (Photo by Richard Bram, courtesy Derby Festival)

Gladys Knight was grand marshal of the 1993 Pegasus Parade. (Photo by Richard Bram, courtesy Derby Festival)

an excuse to have a party, a grand celebration . . . a happening.

Many of the most recognizable people in the world—politicians, actors, actresses, business leaders, and sports figures—make it a point to show up for the Derby. In 1969, Richard M. Nixon became the first president to attend this ballyhooed race. In 1983, two past presidents—Jimmy Carter and Gerald Ford—and one future chief executive, George Bush, were among the Derby throng.

Very Important People have been a part of the Derby scene for years. Special guests have included Princess Margaret in 1974 and Gen. H. Norman Schwarzkopf in 1991. And then there was comedian Joe E. Brown, who regularly attended the race. "The Kentucky Derby," Brown liked to crack, "is my favorite charity."

The roll call of celebrities appearing in the crowd of 130,594 at the 1994 Derby included Brooke Shields, Jessica Lange, Sam Shepard, Merv Griffin, Dixie Carter, George Strait, Ivana Trump, James Earl Jones, Susan Lucci, Teri Hatcher, Cynthia Geary, and Dennis Hopper. And there was

Gen. H. Norman Schwarzkopf was grand marshal of the 1991 Pegasus Parade. (Photo by Richard Bram, courtesy Derby Festival)

Prince Albert of Monaco, Hugh O'Brian, Pete Rose, Dwight Yoakam, Dennis Cole, Steve Guttenberg, Tonya Walker, Doug Stone, Arte Johnson, Woody Harrelson, former Dallas Cowboys coach Jimmy Johnson, and Wendy's founder, Dave Thomas. Secretary of the Treasury Lloyd Bentsen and his wife, B.A., also were part of the Derby scene, as were Gary Collins and his wife, former Miss America Mary Ann Mobley.

Also in the crowd were three well-known owners of '94 Derby starters. Movie producer Albert J. ("Cubby") Broccoli and his wife, Dana, were represented with Brocco, who finished fourth; songwriter Burt Bacharach's Soul of the Matter ran fifth; and Motown Records founder Berry Gordy's Powis Castle came in eighth.

The Derby attracts big people, and it generates big numbers. In 1994, a total of $45,419,406 was wagered on the Derby from in-state, national, and international sources, including $7,449,744 at Churchill Downs. Besides those wagers, there are all those office pools on the Derby throughout the country. People who don't know a fetlock from a furlong suddenly become interested in horse racing when the Derby rolls around each spring.

The magic of America's most celebrated horse race is impossible to put into words. The printed word is merely ink on paper. The Derby is so much more than that. It's full of life, exuberance, excitement. If a single word could begin to describe the Derby, it's this one: overwhelming.

Famed country philosopher Irvin S. Cobb of Paducah, Ky., was a man gifted with words, but he said he couldn't explain the Derby's magic. "If I could do that, I'd have a larynx of spun silver and the tongue of an angel," he said.

Cobb added: "Until you go to Kentucky and with your own eyes behold the Derby, you ain't never been nowheres and you ain't never seen nothin'!"

In 1956, John Steinbeck wrote: "This Kentucky Derby, whatever it is—a race, an emotion, a turbulence, an explosion—is one of the most beautiful and violent and satisfying things I have ever experienced."

The Derby, which has been held at historic Churchill Downs since 1875 and was first called the "Run for the Roses" in the mid-1920s, has attracted a crowd in excess of 100,000 every year beginning in 1969. The record Derby attendance was the 163,628 that turned out for the 100th running in 1974. A record field of twenty-three also started in that Derby, which was won by Cannonade.

Cannonade was trained by Hall of Famer W. C. ("Woody") Stephens, a man who later would pull off a remarkable feat by conditioning five straight winners of the Belmont Stakes—Conquistador Cielo (1982), Caveat (1983), Swale (1984), Creme Fraiche (1985), and Danzig Connection (1986). Over the years, Stephens has made a big name for himself in New York, but he's a native Kentuckian and he remembers his roots. Ask him to name his biggest thrill in racing and he'll reply: "The 100th Derby, in front of the home folks, down home. The five Belmonts are beautiful, but I can never forget the one back home, the 100th Derby. I won it in front of the home folks. That was a mighty big afternoon."

The Kentucky Derby, a race for three-year-olds, was patterned after the Epsom Derby in England and was contested at a mile and one-half from 1875 through 1895. For its 1896 running, the Derby was shortened to its current distance of a mile and one-quarter. The race has been held on the first Saturday in May each year since 1938, with the exception of 1945, when it was run on June 9 due to a wartime ban on racing in the United States lasting for four months until May 8.

Many champion racehorses have competed in the Churchill Downs classic, including eleven winners of the Triple Crown (Kentucky Derby, Preakness, and Belmont). Those eleven are Sir Barton (1919), Gallant Fox (1930), Omaha (1935), War Admiral (1937), Whirlaway (1941), Count Fleet (1943), Assault (1946), Citation (1948), Secretariat (1973), Seattle Slew (1977), and Affirmed (1978). Besides these champions, other outstanding horses who've won the Derby include Hindoo (1881), Old Rosebud (1914), Exterminator (1918), Twenty Grand (1931), Cavalcade

(1934), Swaps (1955), Carry Back (1961), Northern Dancer (1964), Majestic Prince (1969), Spectacular Bid (1979), Alysheba (1987), and Sunday Silence (1989). Three fillies—Regret (1915), Genuine Risk (1980), and Winning Colors (1988)—have captured the Derby.

Calumet Farm, located near Lexington, has owned more Derby winners (eight) than any other stable. Ben A. Jones trained a record six Derby winners, all but one for Calumet. Eddie Arcaro and Bill Hartack each rode five winners of the Derby, a record. Secretariat ran the fastest Derby of all time—1:59⅖.

One of the cherished moments in Derby history came in 1990 when trainer Carl Nafzger, a former rodeo bull rider, described the race to Frances A. Genter, the ninety-two-year-old owner of Unbridled, from a box at the Downs. This Grand Old Lady of Racing had been involved in the sport for a half-century, and Unbridled was her first Derby starter. In an emotional scene that Hollywood couldn't have improved on, Nafzger excitedly exclaimed: "He's taking the lead! He's gonna win! He's gonna win! He's gonna win! He's a winner! He's a winner, Mrs. Genter!

"You've won the Kentucky Derby, Mrs. Genter. I love you."

Jockey Pat Day had a choice between Unbridled and runner-up Summer Squall, and he had picked the latter. Afterward, in the jockeys' room, he described watching Nafzger on the television rerun. "Keeping Mrs. Genter abreast of where their colt was brought tears to my eyes. She's been in the business a long time, and I congratulate her. I couldn't understand why I lost until I saw Mrs. Genter win. Maybe it just wasn't meant for us to win today. It was obviously meant for her to win."

The Unbridled story is part of the lore of the Derby, a race steeped in tradition. The Derby is such a popular event that approximately 1,800 press credentials are issued to writers, editors, photographers, and members of the electronic media. For years, many of the greatest names in journalism have come to Louisville to try to capture the essence of this race.

In the *1986 Kentucky Derby Souvenir Magazine,* the gifted Dave Kindred wrote: "I am asked to place the Kentucky Derby among the world's extraordinary sports events. I have worked at the World Series and Super Bowl. I have seen the Masters. Both summer and winter, I have gone to the Olympics. I have been to South Bend for football and Lexington for basketball. I knew Muhammad Ali at his best. These pins I place in a sporting map as reference for the reader because otherwise it is without meaning when I say the Kentucky Derby stands alone.

"There lives with this simple horse race a romance that is gone from other games. We see in baseball and football the advent of corporate giants as owners of pitchers and quarterbacks who are themselves corporations. These are bloodless times, though in the rush of events we can forget that. Immersion in Wimbledon and Indianapolis may persuade us that a sporting joy yet lives. It is only by returning to Louisville that we know true delight."

Furman Bisher, sports editor of *The Atlanta Journal,* has covered forty-five straight runnings of the Kentucky Derby, and he, too, writes in glowing terms of this race's magnitude. "The Derby has no detractors," Bisher wrote in the *1994 Kentucky Derby Official Souvenir Magazine.* "It is everybody's game. The disgustingly wealthy, the nouveau riche, the average guy, the good, the bad, the ugly and the beautiful. Every red-blooded American grows up dedicated to seeing one Kentucky Derby. It is more than a tradition, more than a Super Bowl or a Masters. At the Derby, you are not only spectator, you can be one of the players. You may not touch a mint julep—I never was much for weeds in my booze—or even touch a horse, but for one full day, you are part of a kind of scene that makes you feel like you're acting in a movie."

Kentucky, of course, is known far and wide for its horses, and natives of the Bluegrass State indeed do take great pride in the heritage of the noble Thoroughbred.

Kentucky boasts many of the most famous, the most beautiful, and the most tradition-rich farms to be found in the world. There's Calumet Farm with its gleaming white fences and green, lush pastures; Claiborne Farm with its natural beauty and its blue-blooded stallions; Three Chimneys Farm with Seattle Slew and other prominent horses on its stallion roster; Hamburg Place with its great heritage stemming back to noted horseman John E. Madden, "The Wizard of the Turf"; Lane's End Farm, where Queen Elizabeth II has stayed during her visits to Kentucky; and Gainesway Farm with its stud barns fit for royalty.

The Thoroughbred, of course, is treated like royalty in Kentucky, occupying a prominent place in the state's economic, social, and sports worlds. Why so? Why did Kentucky become so identified with Thoroughbreds? Why did this state develop into the best place in the world to breed them?

A major reason is the phosphatic limestone in the fertile soil of central Kentucky, all the better to build strong bones in racehorses. Joe Estes, the late editor of *The Blood-Horse* magazine, once added another key factor into this equation, writing: "It was to be found neither in the nature of the country nor in the heritage of Thoroughbred blood, but in the character of the people who came to be called Kentuckians. Such was their heritage, from the colonies to the east and from their ancestral background in England, that they needed action, adventure, creation, conquest—the Alpine heights of life. When there were no Indians to be chased there were arguments to be settled, and in Kentucky it usually takes a horse race to settle an argument."

Kentuckians do love their horses, and when the Derby rolls around each spring, they love to party, too. The parties abound in Kentucky at Derbytime. The Derby Festival's most elegant affair is the Fillies Derby Ball, at which a spin of the wheel determines the Festival Queen among five finalists.

The Kentucky Derby Museum Gala is a charity ball held in the Churchill Downs infield.

On Derby Eve, certain traditional parties are held in Kentucky, including bashes held by Marylou Whitney in Lexington, Anita Madden in Lexington, and the Diamond

Derby Celebrity Gala hosted by Dr. David E. Brown and his wife, Tricia Barnstable Brown, in Louisville.

Louisvillians, showing their finest Southern hospitality, try their best to roll out the red carpet for the thousands of Derby visitors. In 1993, veteran sportswriter John Crittenden, in his first trip to Louisville, covered the Kentucky Derby, and he couldn't help but be impressed by, among other things, the way people courteously went out of their way to give him directions and make his stay in his hotel as comfortable as possible.

Crittenden, racing writer for *The Palm Beach Post,* would recall: "The 1993 Kentucky Derby lasted two minutes. I was in Louisville four days. I will remember the horse race. Longer, I will remember the special way I was treated. I did feel like a guest."

2

Eddie Sweat: One Man's Love for Secretariat

EDDIE SWEAT HAS SPENT most of his life around horses. But not just ordinary horses. He may be the most famous groom in the history of North American racing.

During his career on the racetrack, he has groomed two Kentucky Derby winners—Riva Ridge in 1972 and Secretariat in 1973. Those two horses were favored to win the Derby, as was another horse groomed by Sweat—Chief's Crown, who finished third in the 1985 renewal. All three were champions. Secretariat was Horse of the Year in 1972 and 1973, and Riva Ridge and Chief's Crown were champion two-year-old colts in 1971 and 1984, respectively.

Sweat also has appeared on the Derby scene as groom for Amberoid, seventh in 1966, and Dike, third in 1969.

Secretariat, Riva Ridge, Dike, and Amberoid all were trained by Lucien Laurin. Chief's Crown was trained by Laurin's son, Roger.

In the early summer of 1993, we sat down with Sweat in a tack room at Churchill Downs while he reflected on Secretariat. The fifty-three-year-old groom was closer to this great horse during his racing days than anybody—closer to him

Groom Eddie Sweat held Secretariat in the winner's circle following the colt's track-record victory in the 1973 Kentucky Derby. Ron Turcotte was aboard Secretariat. (© 1973 Churchill Downs Incorporated/Kinetic Corporation)

than Laurin, than jockey Ron Turcotte, than owner Penny Tweedy. Sweat, a good-natured sort who loves his job, discussed Secretariat's eating and sleeping habits, his great races, his last visit to see the horse, and his love for this famous champion.

Sweat could attest to Secretariat's intelligence. "He was very smart, very smart. As a two-year-old, I think he was a little high-strung, you know, like a little kid. Always bad and always thinks he's tough and always trying to hurt people and all that. His whole life changed from two to three. After he growed up and he raced so many times and he know what racing was all about—and 'I'm not supposed to be fighting nobody no more. All I want to do is run and eat and sleep.' And so that's

what happened. He growed up, and me and him got along just fine. He used to fight me, and I used to fight him *back*, you know, try to teach him, 'You're not supposed to do these things.'

"So he finally realized that, 'Okay, I'll be your brother,'" Sweat added with a chuckle.

Asked if he thought Secretariat loved him the way he loved the horse, Sweat replied: "I think he did. He know me from anybody else. He respected me a lot. If I'd say, 'Get over there, Big Red,' he'd get out of my way. He loved for me to pull on his halter. 'Come on, let's have some fun.' After I'd take his halter off him, I'd pull on it and he'd pull back and I'd pull on it and he'd pull back. I said, 'All right, drop it now, Red. That's enough.' So when he'd turn it loose, I'd throw it in the back of the stall. He'd go back there and pick it up and drop it on the outside. Not supposed to be in here. That's how smart he was. Very smart horse. Most of them horses would be chewing on it. He would never chew on the leather or anything. I showed Mr. Laurin that one day. He said, 'I ain't looking for no pet. I'm looking for a racehorse. Don't teach him those kind of things.' I said, 'Yes, sir.'

"We used to give him lots of carrots. He wasn't too much of a candy eater. He didn't like too much sweets. But carrots, he'd eat a whole bushel of those. Him and Riva Ridge both. I used to tease both of them—like in the afternoon before time to set their food in, they were right beside each other. I used to have one carrot in each hand. I'd give Secretariat a bite, and Riva Ridge can hear him. He'd be peeping under the hay rack. 'Hey, you gonna give me some?' Then I goes over to him and give him a bite. Then Secretariat gets jealous. So now I give each one of them a carrot apiece. They ain't jealous no more."

Did Secretariat stand or lie down while he was sleeping? "Mostly he was the type of horse who liked to stand up and sleep. But sometimes he'd lay down and stretch his legs out."

Secretariat sometimes appeared arthritic, but Sweat had an answer for that observation. "He was a lefty. He was always like a left-handed person. A lot of people didn't pay attention to that, though. People didn't understand that, they don't believe this. But horses are just like human beings, some of them. Some of them left-handed, some of them is right-handed."

When a horse runs, he reaches out first with one of his forelegs, meaning that he will lead with that leg. Ideally, a horse will lead with his right leg on a straightaway and his left leg on a turn. Sweat said that Secretariat essentially changed leads in the correct fashion in his races. "He'd be on the left (on a turn) and he'd change to the right when you wanted him to change and then he'd go back to his left. Whenever you wanted him to change, he'd do it. He switched leads the right way. Sometimes he was running *so* fast we couldn't hardly tell what kind of lead he was on.

"But he was a lefty, he was. That's what make him look so different from the other horses, and everybody think he was sore. He wasn't sore. That's just the way he was. He used mostly his left, and he switched over to his right, but mostly on his left. And he wasn't no sore horse. That's the awkward way that he traveled.

"People didn't understand. They used to come in and ask me, 'Man, is your horse sore?' I said, 'I don't see anything sore about him. There's a horse ain't never bucked shins.' He tried when he was a two-year-old. He was a little touchy in his shins, but I unbucked him. Mr. Laurin will tell you that. I just worked on him, and it disappeared by treating him with these old lucky hands I got. I used to make my own poultice to pull the soreness or heat or whatever out of a horse's leg. I used to do him up every day with that stuff for about a week. He didn't need it every day, but I did it anyway to make sure. And after that then I started just using a brace. Everything disappeared. We was getting ready to run in the Garden State."

Secretariat won the Garden State Stakes by 3½ lengths to wrap up his two-year-old season with seven victories in nine starts.

Secretariat was a sound horse, but Sweat did note that the colt had "a little splint [a small, round, bony enlargement] on the inside of his leg." Secretariat had won the Garden State Stakes with the splint.

"After he finished his two-year-old campaign," Sweat said, "we decided we would rest him for a month or two down at Hialeah. This little splint popped out, and it was growing. It was just a little, small thing. We caught it before it got too big. Mr. Laurin said, 'Well, I guess we'll take care of that right now. We'll just a put a little fire blister on him while we're laying him up.' That's what we did. We started him back, and by him being so big and strong, his muscles got really tight on him, and it didn't look like we was gonna ever make the Derby with him, the way he was traveling during that time. But his muscles were so tight. When you ain't doing nothin', just walkin', you just get out of shape. It hurts and whatnot. The way he used to go out to the track, he was so stiff.

"Reggie Cornell and a few other trainers said, 'Lucien will never get this horse to the Derby. How can he take a horse to the Derby and he can hardly walk?' They took those words back. It took us a while to get him back in shape, but I think we done a pretty good job at it.

"When we started him back, I used to put Bigeloil, a brace, in the rinsing water and rub him down—his shoulders, his back—and put a heavy blanket on him and let him walk for about twenty minutes with that old, heavy blanket on him, let it soak in good to his muscles, and then we pulled it off. The heavy blanket would keep the heat, and it goes right into the muscles. And then we put a fly net on him, a light piece, for about five, ten minutes—like you put on a light T-shirt or something like that. You could see the difference in him every day. He loosened himself up more and more and more. He started to loosen up day by day. So we finally got him back in shape. Mr. Laurin said, 'Well, I don't think we'll go to the Blue Grass. We'll go to New York, and we'll run him in the Gotham and the Wood Memorial.'"

Secretariat won the Gotham, but then, in his final prep

for the Kentucky Derby, he finished third in the Wood Memorial. It turned out that he ran in the Wood with an abscess under his upper lip. The abscess was detected the morning of the race by Dr. Manuel Gilman, chief veterinarian for New York tracks.

"I didn't know anything about that until Dr. Gilman came around and checked him," Sweat said. "He saw this abscess, and he said, 'Well, maybe the horse, going to have to scratch him.' Mr. Laurin didn't want him to be scratched, and then Mrs. Tweedy said, 'We have to run this horse because of the public. The people want to see him run.' So we take that chance anyway, and we ran him. He finished third. And I think it was bothering him *very much* after that. I don't think Ronnie knew anything about it until after. Ronnie came back and said he was throwing his head, something was bugging him. That's what was bugging him. So now they was undecided about sending him to Churchill Downs for the Derby."

The decision was made to send Secretariat to the Downs, where veterinarian Robert Copelan of Paris, Ky., would check out the abscess.

"Mr. Laurin told me, 'Well, when you get there, let Dr. Copelan take a look at it,'" Sweat recalled. "I saw Dr. Copelan, and he looked at it and he said, 'Well, there's no reason to inject that. All you have to do is put some hot towels on it.' And that's what I started doing. Charlie Davis, the exercise boy, kept bringing hot towels, hot towels, you know. We started around three o'clock that afternoon, and we did it to about five or six o'clock that evening. He ate his dinner that night, but he didn't enjoy it too much. Overnight it just came to a head, and it busted. I guess it was something just like a fever blister, you know. He had a sticker briar that come out of the hay rack probably and stuck in there, and it got infected.

"The next morning I goes out there to give him his breakfast like four o'clock, and I could see all this stuff was splattered on the wall and he was feeling good and yelling for his food and all of that. He was tearing his stall down. He wanted

to eat. He felt *so* good. He was all right after that. He was trying to tell me, 'I feel pretty good.' So I give him the amount of food he was supposed to have, and he ate it up."

Secretariat ran in an entry with Angle Light in the Derby. The entry was favored at 3-2, and there was considerable pressure on the Secretariat camp. The colt, who was coming into the Derby off such a dull effort in the Wood, had been syndicated for a world-record $6.08 million for breeding purposes. The Secretariat people may have felt the pressure, but on that first Saturday in May at Churchill Downs, with the Derby approaching and all the racing world awaiting "the greatest two minutes in sports," Secretariat was snoozing in his stall.

"When they said, 'Get your horses ready for the Kentucky Derby,' he was stretched out in his stall asleep," Sweat recalled. "I had the other horse, Angle Light, ready to go. Charlie Davis took him over to the paddock. So I finally got Secretariat up, and I had to clean him up real quick. On the way, as we were coming around the clubhouse turn, fans were snapping his picture and photographers were there on the track. And he wanted to stand and look at the people and pose for them. And I kept saying, 'Come on, let's go, we're gonna be late.' And Mr. Laurin was getting nervous and everything because I was the last one that came in the paddock. He said, 'Jesus Christ, what happened?' I said, 'I couldn't get him up, and I had to clean him. I had to rush, rush, rush. And *now* he don't want to come over, he just wants to pose for pictures.' He was so nervous, Mr. Laurin, he asked me for a cigarette when he was putting the saddle on him, and he took the whole pack of cigarettes and never give them back to me."

Sweat laughed at the recollection.

"After we got him all saddled up and walking around, now he's getting mad because we had the blinkers on him," Sweat said. "He's ready to go. And they had to wake Ron Turcotte up in the jocks' room. He was asleep also, dreaming that he won the Derby. That's what he told me. On the way out, when we was going out on the track, under the tunnel, he was telling me, 'I was laying in bed sleeping, man. I dreamed

I win the Derby.' I said, 'You're kidding me. I wish to God you do.' I was walking him out on the track, and I said, 'Well, good luck to you, Ron.' And I always gave Secretariat a little pat on his tail when I turned him loose to go out on the track. I said, 'Go get 'em, Big Red.' And that's what he always do. He go get 'em.

"But I was sorta nervous with Secretariat that day—not, say, from the lip or anything like that. I was nervous because he broke dead last, and he was trailing the field. I got awfully nervous. I said, 'I wonder if he can get up in time, you know, to catch Sham.' He was cuttin' them down one, two, three, and four—and he won. I look at the time—59 and 2. I said, 'Well, that was faster than Riva Ridge.'"

Riva Ridge had won the 1972 Derby in 2:01⅘. "He did it all the way in front," Sweat said. "That was a good Derby. That was my first Derby [win], and I was proud to death. But then I was more proud when they came back the next year with Big Red, and he just break the record. That was very great for me.

"I didn't cry, but I was so happy I want to cry. I said, 'Two years in a row, two Derbies in a row.' I was very proud of myself. I was tellin' *me* that. I didn't show it to anybody else."

"And then when he comes back after he wins the race, he *know* when he wins. And I'd be standing out there with my shank, spinning the chain on my finger. And Ron said that when they go into the winner's circle, 'I don't never have to turn this horse. He sees you standing there, and he comes straight to you.' Ron don't have to turn him or nothin'. He come straight to me. He said, 'Well, that's my groom.' Him and Riva Ridge both, they both come right straight to me whenever they win a race."

Champagne was flowing back at Secretariat's barn after the Derby. "There was a lot of celebrating, but, me, I didn't," Sweat said. "I had my mind on taking care of my horses. I had to take care of Angle Light and Secretariat at the same time. I wasn't the groom for Angle Light, but he came along with me and I took care of him. The groom that was taking care of him was back in New York. There wasn't no need to send two grooms. I could take care of him."

Sweat said that between the Wood and Preakness, Secretariat apparently gained weight because his girth changed. "He was wearing a size 48—and that's big as most of the horses is, 46 or 47 or 48. We had to get a size 52 or 52½, somewhere around there. At Pimlico, Charlie Davis came back and said, 'Man, this girth is too tight, it's cutting his breath. We have to get a bigger girth.' The tack people made him another girth, a size 52 or 52½, and I still got that girth. That's the biggest I ever seen. Riva Ridge wore, I think it was a 44, because he wasn't that big in the girth. He had a narrow chest, but he was real powerful behind. After Secretariat ran in the Belmont, that girth was a little bit too loose for him. Then we had to go back to a 48. He lost about fifty-two pounds out of the whole Triple Crown."

Secretariat was a good doer—racetrack parlance meaning that he had a big appetite and would clean up his feed tub. "He was eating sixteen quarts a day—mostly oats, mixed with sweet feed and whatnot," Sweat said. "The average racehorse, if you can get him to eat like ten or twelve quarts a day, that's great. But sixteen quarts a day, that's unbelievable. When I used to give horses like two quarts for breakfast in the morning, I'd give him something like four. Because if I gave him one scoop—that's two quarts, right?—that ain't enough for him. The more he eat, well, the more Mr. Laurin had to train him. He was a very big eater, and he was just putting on weight while he was doing all that training. But Mr. Laurin always tell me, 'Don't feed him so much because he'll get too heavy on me and I'll have to keep training him harder.' But he bugs *me*. He wants to eat, he wants more. And I always slip it and give it to him. That's why I was afraid to tell people how much he eat, and I guess that's what made him a big, strong racehorse.

"When we went to the Preakness, he run a terrific race there. But the Belmont was the most exciting race in my *whole* life, and I've been on the racetrack for quite a few years. And

I never seen a horse that win that far. That day he just break right along with Sham. I guess that was the orders Mr. Laurin told Ron. But we know he was ready for that mile and a half. He said, 'Well, you just stick with Sham. Let's see how far Sham can hold out goin' a mile and a half.' And that's exactly what Ron did. They got to the three-quarter pole, and Sham couldn't take no more. I think he was hurtin' a little bit or somethin'—I don't know. But, anyway, Secretariat just walked away from him and just keep on walkin' away and walkin' away. And I said, 'Oh, no, just don't fall down now, boy.' Tears was comin' from my eyes that day, I was so happy for him."

Secretariat stood his entire stud career at Claiborne Farm, just outside Paris, Ky. When was the last time that Sweat saw Secretariat?

"I think it was the time when we retired Chief's Crown. I think it was '85. I spent three days with him on Three Chimneys Farm, so one day I went over and that's the last I saw him. He was way over in the paddock. I made a funny noise like a duck. Him and Riva Ridge both understood that noise that I made. The stud man was there, the manager. He said, 'Come on, champ.' He knew the stud man, too. And then he saw me. He lifted his head up, and he come walking very slowly to the fence. He rolled his eyes at me and he said, 'I remember that voice.' That was so great that day. It made me feel so good, you know. I say, 'I think he still remember me'—you know, that voice that I'd make. I say, 'You remember when you win the Belmont by 31 lengths?' And he started to gnaw on the fence. Like he was saying, 'Yeah, I remember that.' So I patted on the head, and I said, 'Well, okay, champ, I gotta go now.' I said, 'I'll see you around sometime.' He just turned away and walked on back over in the centerfield and started eating. I said, 'That's great.' He looked beautiful. He was great."

Secretariat, suffering from laminitis, was humanely destroyed on October 4, 1989. Sweat was in Canada when he heard the news of Secretariat's death in Kentucky.

It was Secretariat by an incredible 31 lengths in the 1973 Belmont Stakes. (Courtesy New York Racing Association)

Groom Eddie Sweat held Secretariat at Belmont Park as trainer Lucien Laurin, jockey Ron Turcotte, and owner Penny Tweedy looked on. (Courtesy New York Racing Association)

"I didn't know anything about it until I saw the reporters was coming around the barn with the cameras and all that," Sweat recalled. "They said, 'You heard about Secretariat?' I said, 'No. What happened?' 'They had to put him down.' And quite a few other people told me the same thing. I didn't know until that very day. I was very upset. It took me at least a month or so to get over that because I was just thinking about him. I said, 'Gee, when I get back to Kentucky, I want to go over and see him.' And he died. So I told the people up there that it was a very, very shocking thing to me because I was so close to him at the time that he was racing, and he was a horse I would never forget. I probably will never get another one like him. If I have one just half as good as him, I will be a happy, little man right now.

"I loved him and Riva Ridge both—and Chief's Crown. I stuck with them. I put all my efforts in all of those horses. They never go no place. I just stayed around the barn and watched them. I was always there. Them horses was part of my life. They was making a living for me, and I was making a living for them. I made sure they got their food on the right schedule. I checked them out to see if they got any cuts or bruises or anything. I was like *everything* to those horses—every horse that I take care of you got to make sure because you don't want to see anything happen to them."

In the spring of 1993, Sweat visited the graves of Secretariat and Riva Ridge at Claiborne.

"Me and Roger Laurin's son, Robert, we went and checked all the old horses. We went to Claiborne Farm and visited his grave and Riva Ridge's. I put a little flower on both of their graves. Then we went over to see Chief's Crown at Three Chimneys. He was just getting ready to go to the stud barn, and he didn't pay me any mind. Then we went over to see the little babies that Chief's Crown had. It was fun that day."

Sweat had a nickname for Secretariat—Big Red. "That's all we ever did call call him—Big Red, after Man o' War."

Those two legendary racehorses each ran twenty-one

times in their careers. Secretariat won sixteen races, Man o' War twenty.

Sweat called Secretariat the greatest horse in his lifetime and likely in a lot of other people's lifetimes, also. "He was very great. Anything you asked this horse to do, he would do it. If you wanted him to go slow, he'd go slow. If you wanted him to go fast, he'd go faster and faster and faster. And the faster he run, the *more* he want to run, you know. Just like Ron told me, he said, 'You know something, Sweat? I don't even know how fast this horse can run.' He told everybody that. He said, 'When I ask him, he picks up more—and more.' So I guess we will never know how fast he could run. I don't know about Man o' War because that was *way* before my time. I wasn't even existing in this world. But I know how fast he could run by reading up on him. He was a pretty nice horse. He was a world-beater."

Will Harbut, longtime stud groom for Man o' War, liked to say that celebrated runner was "the mostest hoss dat ever was." If Harbut were still alive and said that his horse was "the mostest hoss dat ever was," what would Sweat say in reply? "Well, I would tell him, I rubbed one, too, that was just as big as he was.'

"I would tell him that. Maybe we might get in a little argument about it," Sweat went on, chuckling, "but I *would* tell him because I think Secretariat was *just as good* as Man o' War. There's no doubt in my mind. I mean, he could run just as fast as Man o' War could."

John Wayne, grand marshal of the 1976 Pegasus Parade, waved to the crowd. (Courtesy *The Courier-Journal*)

3

"The Duke" at the Derby

Aug. 13, 1976

Dear Jack,

A hearty thanks to you for the wonderful way that we were treated at the 102nd running of the Kentucky Derby. I hope Louisville is as proud of you as they should be. Your tips to me at the Derby prove that the races have to be on the level.

Warm regards, John Wayne.
(Signed "Duke")

HE CAME TO THE DERBY, and even if he may not have won money at the races, he won the hearts of Kentuckians. John Wayne, "the Duke" himself, was the grand marshal of the Pegasus Parade and attended the Derby in 1976.

Through the efforts of two men who were connected with the Kentucky Derby Festival at the time—executive vice-president Jack Guthrie and director Jeff Davidson (chairman of the celebrity committee)—it was arranged for Wayne to come to the Derby. "I thought with the '76 Derby—the nation's bicentennial, and red, white, and blue—let's go for 'the Duke,'" Guthrie recalled. "Who better represents the spirit of America? The only thing he could say was no—if I could just get to him."

Davidson, who was the president and general manager of WLKY-TV in Louisville at the time, played a major role in landing "the Duke" for the Derby Festival. It seems that Davidson was a friend of Dick Colbert, the head of a major television syndication company with offices located on the same floor as those of Wayne's Batjac Productions in California. Colbert put one of Wayne's sons, Michael, the business man at Batjac, in touch with Davidson and Guthrie, one thing led to another, and arrangements were made for "the Duke" to attend the '76 Derby.

Guthrie and Davidson both have fond recollections of Wayne's visit to the Derby. The letter to Guthrie hangs on his office wall in Louisville. As for Davidson, he struck up a friendship with Wayne at the Derby that lasted for the rest of the actor's life. "My mother kept John Wayne supplied with her strawberry jam for as long as he lived," Davidson said.

The Derby traditionally attracts celebrities galore, but through the course of the race's history, few have been more popular than Wayne, truly an American institution.

Those who came in contact with Wayne at the '76 Derby remember him for many things—his genuine qualities, his taste for tequila, and his interest in the Derby. Wayne and his entourage arrived in Louisville by a private jet, and Kentuckians rolled out the red carpet for this legend. He was put up in the exclusive Presidential Suite on the twenty-fifth floor of The Galt House, compliments of the hotel's owner, Al Schneider. People greeted Wayne with signs from windows in a building (then known as the Louisville Trust Building) next to The Galt House:

> Hello, Duke
> Welcome to Louisville
> We Love You, Duke
> Welcome, Duke, to Kentucky
> Have a Great Derby
> Wave to Us, Duke

Wayne waved to his fans standing at the windows. "He got a

big kick out of it," recalled Tom O'Hearn, The Galt House general manager. "I think he was kinda surprised when he looked out.

"He was extremely outgoing and warm, extremely friendly, and extremely humble," O'Hearn added. "I was expecting something completely different."

Wayne was interviewed by a television station on the Belvedere in downtown Louisville. A large crowd was on hand for an activity, and many of the people naturally wanted to get close to Duke.

"We were together," Guthrie recalled, "and he said, 'Keep moving. I'll stay with you.' I said, 'Fine.' He would pat the kids on the head or he'd hand out little cards with his autograph on them. They'd want an autograph, and he said, 'Haven't got time for that—but, here, have one of these.' He kept a bunch of them in his pocket.

"When we got back upstairs in The Galt House, he said, 'Don't think I'm being impolite. I'm big enough—nobody's going to hurt me—but when I go some places sometimes it does draw a crowd and if a little child was trying to get up to me and fell and got hurt, I would never forgive myself. The last thing I want to see is somebody get hurt. I'll hand these cards out. I don't mind meeting and talking to anybody, but I don't like crowds to form because we then don't have control of the situation.'"

Wayne also explained another one of his concerns that he had in public—or rather in the privacy of a rest room. "When we'd go someplace and he'd go to the rest room, he'd go in the stall," Guthrie said. "He'd never stand there at the urinal. I never thought anything about it. At times, he would explain why he did something, and he said, 'I'm sure you've noticed I don't go up to the urinal. I go into the stall.' I said, 'Whatever you want to do.' He said, 'Well, let me tell you, years and years ago, after people began to know who I was, on three different occasions I'd go up and I'd be standing there and somebody would look up to me and say, "My, God, you're John Wayne."'"

Wayne proceeded to explain that, in these situations, the person noticing him would turn to his direction and—well, you get the picture. Needless to say, three such experiences—and several dry-cleaning bills—were enough to convince Wayne to head for the stall when he entered a rest room.

Kentucky is well known for its bourbon, but Wayne preferred another type of drink. "He drank a fifth of tequila a day," Guthrie said. "But you'd never know it. He'd pour it over rocks or he'd drink it straight up. The rest of us drank our bourbon, but he liked his tequila."

"I had ordered a case of Jose Cuervo tequila at his suite in The Galt House," Davidson said. "I said to him, 'They tell me you drink tequila.' He said, 'Yeah. I don't mean to insult you, but I've got my own. Would you like one?' I said, 'Certainly.' His secretary, Pat Stacy, was with him and a guy by the name of Barney Fotheringham, who was sort of his lieutenant to do anything he wanted done. So he sent Barney to get some tequila, and he brought out a thing called Sauza Conmemorativo in a brown bottle. He said, 'That's what I drink. Let me fix you one.' So he took one of those great big lowball glasses, filled it full of ice, filled it up with tequila, put a lemon on top of it, smashed it down with that big hand on top of the ice, and said, 'Let it sit for about a minute.' I said, 'Do you use any salt?' He said, 'You won't need any.' And that's what I have consumed in the way of tequila ever since."

On Thursday of Derby Week, Wayne served as grand marshal of the Pegasus Parade. John Filiatreau wrote in *The Courier-Journal:* "[The parade] strutted through downtown Louisville under clear skies and in perfect shirtsleeve weather, transforming the city into a carnival of Derbytime sights and smells. A crowd estimated at more than 100,000 lined the parade route, while untold others watched through the windows of nearby buildings, perched on fire escapes and sat atop roofs."

In *The Louisville Times,* Meredith McGrath reported that

1,776 marching teen-agers, wearing red, white, and blue T-shirts, represented "The Spirit of '76," a band of Southern Indiana junior and senior high school students. McGrath wrote that after lining up for the start of the parade, "in the best Cecil B. DeMille tradition, the Red, White and Blue Sea of T-shirts parted to make way for John Wayne." McGrath continued, "Wayne was to precede the band as it rolled down Broadway. He waited until after the band had already covered the street before he rode in his convertible at the head of the line. And when it was time for his arrival, the kids broke ranks. The teens raised a cheer and rushed to the center of the street to catch a glimpse of Wayne in his big white cowboy hat. They weren't disappointed, for it was about five more minutes before the parade began, and they and the people lining the block got an extra long look at the star. 'Hell, he looks the same as ever. He doesn't look any different. See, look at him laughing,' commented one man."

Wayne seemed to thoroughly enjoy himself in Kentucky during this festive time. One evening he and his group went to Min's Steakhouse (today it's called Pat's Steakhouse), a popular Louisville restaurant frequented by horse people. Henry Wolf, who was one of the waiters serving the party, would always remember that a member of Wayne's entourage brought a briefcase with a bottle of tequila in it. "They asked us just to bring a bowl of ice and a bowl of lemons," Wolf recalled, "and John Wayne was drinking tequila out of an iced-tea glass.

"He was real congenial," added Wolf, now the manager at Pat's. "He was kind of quiet, I thought. He just observed everybody."

Bridget Sherrill, a longtime Derby Festival employee, recalled the down-to-earth qualities of Wayne. "He came to the Festival office," said Sherrill, a bookkeeper at the time. "As he was leaving, I said, 'Oh, gosh, I wish you would call my children and talk to them. That would really be neat.' He said, okay, he would do it. I dialed the number, and he took the time to talk to my children [Lisa, ten, and Todd, eight] on the phone. Like, 'Hi, this is John Wayne'—and that kind of thing. Lisa answered the phone, and Todd got on the extension. At the time, I was real hoarse, and he told them I had been drinking. Then he laughed, and they knew that he wasn't serious. That was very, very nice. That seemed like the kind of person that he was. When you think of him, you think of him as this huge man, this man with power and everything like that—that he wouldn't be that personable. But he was."

The day before the Derby, Wayne and a group of people went to central Kentucky to visit such showcase Thoroughbred nurseries as Claiborne Farm and Calumet Farm. "We took three cars," Guthrie said. "Davidson and I were in the one with Wayne. We put some sandwiches and beer in the trunk—just going to make a day of it. It was interesting just being with him—what you saw on the screen was the same thing you saw in person. He was just John Wayne. We listened to numerous personal stories and heard some of his conservative views regarding the current political scene."

The Claiborne people never have forgotten Wayne's visit. To this day, Claiborne president Seth Hancock has a photograph of himself with Wayne under a glass on his desk. "He was a very, very nice man," said Hancock, who personally took Wayne and the group on a tour to see a few stallions, including 1973 Triple Crown champion Secretariat. "I always liked him in the movies, but I liked him even better just what little time I was around him. He was just a regular guy, I thought. He was in the flesh like you would imagine he'd be—kind of a big, tough guy and voice like you would expect. I'd say he was a real man's man. It's hard to form an opinion on somebody over a half-hour, but I was real impressed with him."

Claiborne manager John Sosby was equally impressed. "John Wayne was always my hero," Sosby recalled. "He did everything right. Always made the good movies. He was always the good guy. Got beat up and shot sometimes—but always won the girl or won the battle. While he was here, he

John Wayne and Jack Guthrie, then executive vice-president of the Kentucky Derby Festival, with Secretariat at Claiborne Farm. (Photo by Buck Peters)

was joshing around. He was just real nice to be around. He was just full of enjoyment."

Joe B. Hall, the University of Kentucky basketball coach at the time, was at Claiborne on this occasion. Guthrie, a UK graduate and fan, noticed Hall watching from a distance next to a tree by the side of a farm road, and invited him over to meet Wayne.

Wayne was happy to pose for pictures at Claiborne. "There's one shot that I remember he took with all the farmhands," Guthrie said. "He knelt down in the center, and they all got around him. He was just a nice guy. He didn't care whether you were cleaning out the stalls or whether your name was Seth Hancock, everyone was the same. And Seth made sure everybody got to meet him."

After leaving Claiborne, the group headed for Calumet. Guthrie recalled that Adm. Gene Markey, husband of Calumet owner Lucille Markey, had financed one of John

Wayne's early movies. "[Wayne] said they had corresponded every so often through the years. He knew Admiral Markey was getting up there in age, and he wanted to go to Calumet."

Wayne & Co. had lunch along the way from Claiborne to Calumet, but it wasn't at a fancy restaurant. "We were on an interstate," Guthrie recalled, "and he said, 'Well, why don't we stop for lunch?' I said, 'I don't know whether we're supposed to. I don't think it's legal.' He said, 'Well, who's gonna stop us?' So we pulled over—all three cars—on the side of the road, not in a rest area, and we popped the trunk that had the beer and the sandwiches, and we were all standing around on the side of the road with a ham sandwich and a beer. Everybody's got their foot up on the bumper, telling some stories and chugging a beer. Can't you imagine if you were on vacation and driving down the interstate—'Hey, Mabel. Mabel, God, do you know who that was with a beer in his hand on the side of the road?'"

Ol' Mabel would never have believed whom she just went by on that Kentucky road.

While at Calumet, Stacy and Davidson accompanied Wayne into the farm's mansion for his visit with Markey. "Gene Markey and Duke belonged to the Balboa Yacht Club, which was a very small group—a very close confederation of a few friends," Davidson said. "Gene and his wife both were rather along in years and using canes. Gene pushed a little button on a cord, and servants came from everywhere."

The sixty-eight-year-old Wayne wasn't in the best of health at the time—he died in 1979 of complications from cancer—but he was in the best of spirits. Guthrie recalled that when he entered Wayne's bedroom at The Galt House to gather some papers, he couldn't help but make certain observations. "He sent in all of his breathing apparatus—oxygen tanks and all," Guthrie said. "He must have had six pillows stacked up on his bed. So I'm assuming that he must have slept almost sitting straight up."

Guthrie marveled at how Wayne, despite his health problems, kept going without complaining, without making excuses, without wanting people to feel sorry for him. He had recently finished a movie called *The Shootist,* which starred the actor as a gunfighter dying of cancer. Wayne himself had had half a lung removed for cancer.

Initial arrangements were for the Derby Festival to pick up Wayne's expenses, but "the Duke" would have nothing to do with that idea. "I was in the suite reviewing with Barney Fotheringham some of the expenses that we were going to take care of," Guthrie recalled. "John overheard some of our conversation, and he came over and said, 'What are you all doing?' We told him, and he looked at Barney and said, 'No, let the studio pick it up. We can do it better than the Festival can. I'd rather pick up the costs. I've had a good time here. They've been great to us.'

"It was a nice gesture on his behalf," Guthrie added.

Wayne attended the Derby as the guest of Al Schneider. "He said he'd never had a police escort before," Guthrie recalled. "We got him a police escort—the first one he had was coming in from the airport downtown and then we had one on Derby Day to go to the track, and, of course, that *is* the way to go to the track. You go up on sidewalks and down and around and what have you. He said, 'This police escort was the most fun I've had in years.'"

At the track, people yelled to Wayne: "Duke, hey, Duke." One man asked, "Where are the wagons, Duke?"

"The actor shook hands, signed autographs and then went upstairs to one of the glass-enclosed areas set aside for those who are willing to pay dearly for watching the Derby," Dick Kaukas wrote in *The Courier-Journal.*

After the Derby, Wayne went to Davidson's house for a private party that evening. Davidson insisted that no pictures be taken at the party. "One of my neighbors slipped in with a camera," he said with a chuckle, "and I made her take her camera home."

The Davidson party was a fun affair. "Duke said, 'Look, it's Pat's birthday—we need a place to ice down some champagne,'" Davidson recalled. "I said, 'That's easy to do.' He said, 'Well, I got a big bottle.' He had a double jeroboam of Mumms Cordon Rouge champagne. It was so damn big we couldn't find a cooler to put it in, so we put it in one of the bathtubs at the house and iced it down. It would honestly stand probably four feet tall. So we iced it down, and he gave Pat a present. Then we started drinking the champagne. Finally, he decided he wanted to go to the hotel, and I took him back. I came back, and about that time I heard this big boom, boom, boom on the back door of the house and it's Hal Linden with a baseball bat that somebody had given him. He wanted to see John Wayne, but he missed him."

Before leaving Louisville the day after the Derby, Wayne told The Galt House's O'Hearn how special the trip had been to him. "He remarked about how he really enjoyed the spirit of the event and how much the Derby meant to America," O'Hearn said. "I thought it was pretty touching. I was taken by his knowledge of the Derby and how he felt the emotion and how he got into it and how much he really enjoyed Derby Day. He just was effusive in his praise about his cordial reception and how historic and beautiful Churchill Downs was."

Wayne repaid Schneider in a very special way for his hospitality at The Galt House and at the Derby. "He was thanking Al for his generosity," Guthrie recalled. "He said, 'What do I give somebody like you to show my appreciation?' He paused and said, 'Well, I've got an idea.' He had on a big ten-gallon hat, and he took it off his head and put it on Schneider's head. And Schneider looked like a little kid who just got every piece of candy he could get out of the candy store."

After all these years, Schneider still treasures the hat.

Guthrie said that, to his knowledge, the '76 Derby was Wayne's only trip to the Run for the Roses.

Davidson best summed up the feelings of those who met John Wayne on his visit to the '76 Derby. "He was a marvelous, marvelous individual," Davidson said. "He was one of the nicest people you ever saw. Could be very, very strong in his beliefs, but he was a wonderful, wonderful man."

4

Carry Back: The People's Choice

IN 1981, SEATED IN HER Churchill Downs clubhouse box on the twenty-year anniversary of the '61 Kentucky Derby, Katherine Price listened to a tape recording of television announcer Bryan Field's call of Carry Back's stirring come-from-behind victory.

Carry Back charged from more than 13 lengths behind at the quarter pole to win the Derby by three-quarters of a length.

What remembrances did the call of the race bring back to Mrs. Price, the owner of Carry Back and the wife of the colt's trainer and breeder, Jack? "I realize how foolish I was, because I was so sure we'd win the race," she said. "But now that I'm more experienced, I realize how naïve I was. You know, it was pure stupidity.

"I was amazed at everybody making such a big thing over it," she said. "I guess that's because I have been to the Derby a number of times but had never been a participant. So I couldn't get over the way people felt towards it, but it didn't hit me until after I had gone home and found all the fan mail—from Tokyo, from Peru, from everywhere. That's when it really hit me."

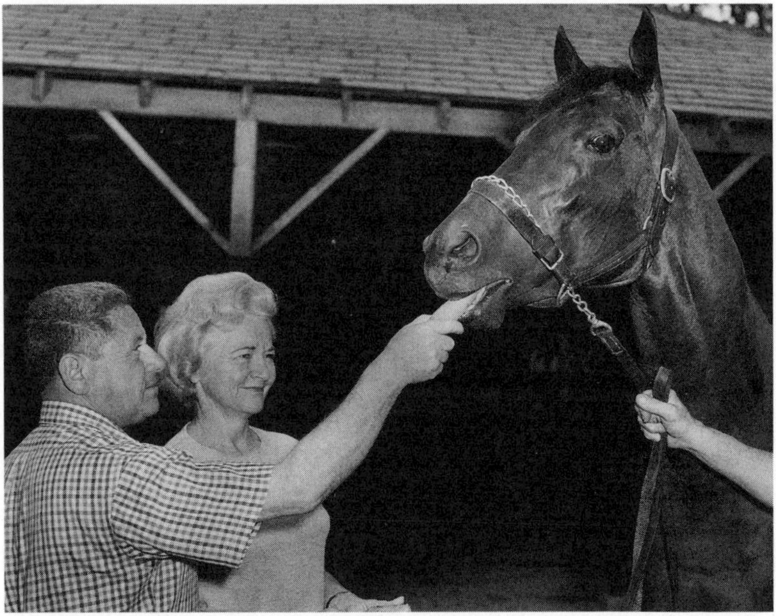

Jack Price fed Carry Back a carrot as Katherine looked on at Saratoga in 1962. (Courtesy Jack Price collection)

She remembered that immediately after the race she turned and all but apologized to some nearby owners who had starters in the race.

"I said, 'I'm sorry.' But I couldn't get their attention, because their faces were so long like it was a fixed race or something, like they were supposed to win. They had long shots in the race. We had the favorite. I thought to myself, they don't deserve my sympathy. I was going to say, 'Tomorrow's another day' or something like that and instead said, 'I'm sorry.' And they didn't even recognize me."

The horses owned by those people have long since been forgotten, but Carry Back earned his place in racing history. This 1961 champion three-year-old colt was named to racing's Hall of Fame, quite an honor for any horse, especially one that came from a union that cost no more than $665. Breeders like to say, "Breed the best to the best and hope for the best." Jack Price did something like that, and he came up with Carry Back. He bred the best he had to the best he could afford.

The best he had was a trio of mares that included Joppy, who frequently was referred to as having cost Price $300 (half of which reportedly came from an overdue board bill owed him by her previous owner) but who apparently was actually acquired for $265 (a $150 cash outlay plus the cancellation of a $115 board bill). He bred the three mares to the best he could afford, a sire named Saggy who was standing at Country Life Farm in Maryland. The stud fee was $400. Actually, Saggy stood for $750, but Price received a discount by breeding three mares to the stallion.

Fourleafclover, one of the mares, produced a filly named Could Mean Luck. She never won in twenty starts. Paigle, another of the mares, had a defective foal and it died.

And then there was the unheralded Joppy, who foaled Carry Back at the Ocala Stud in Florida. A mating between Joppy and Saggy was not expected to turn out anything special. Instead, it produced a champion named Carry Back.

Carry Back, who raced in either Katherine's name or for the Prices' Dorchester Farm Stable, earned $1,241,165 in purses. In addition, he brought home at least $500,000 in stud fees for the Prices.

Carry Back obviously didn't represent the blue bloods, but he outran them time and again. And Jack Price enjoyed himself along the way. Indeed, few people have ever had more fun with a horse than did Jack and Katherine Price with Carry Back. "He was a member of the family," Jack said.

Price, a professional horseman and amateur comedian, liked to poke fun at some of racing's traditions. It was Jack Price against the Establishment's stuffed shirts, many of whom considered it sacrilegious to laugh.

The Kentucky Derby is the sport's most glamorous, most publicized, most ballyhooed horse race. But Jack Price told everybody in '61 that it was nothing more than the seventh race on the first Saturday in May at Churchill Downs.

"People talk about the glory and sentiment attracted to the Derby, but I have my own ideas on that subject," Price said. "I suspect that when Wathen Knebelkamp [the Churchill Downs president] wipes the tears from his eyes as the band plays 'My Old Kentucky Home,' he also looks across at the odds board to see if this year's money handle is as high as last year's."

Price made some other remarks about the hallowed Bluegrass institution. He said the Derby would be nice to win for Carry Back's sake, but he personally didn't give a damn about the race. The purse money, Price maintained, was his chief reason for running Carry Back in the Derby.

Price was "mostly kidding" when he said those things about the Derby, but a lot of Kentuckians thought he should forget about making jokes and stick to training horses—preferably in another state. Price may have irritated some hardboots in 1961, but actually he was a refreshing breeze on the Derby scene. His candid comments pumped new life into the old sport.

Before he left Louisville, Price denied that he had been touched in any way by the tradition of the Derby. "I still think it's just another race," he said. "I almost went to sleep two hours before the race and had to take a pep-up pill."

Price was more than a talker. He was a sound, knowledgeable racing man. When Carry Back came along, Price struck it rich.

Looking back on the 1961 Derby, Price once said, "First, never having had or even hoped to have a horse of the caliber of Carry Back, we did not have a master plan, such as many owners and trainers have when their main objective is to win the Derby. Don't forget, I didn't have a lot of money or a large income, so our objective was to win as much as possible without hurting the horse. The Derby was just another race in his busy schedule. After Carry Back won, I realized how important the Derby victory was to his career as a stallion."

And Price remains one of the Derby's most loyal supporters, returning year after year although he is bringing nothing on four legs to the Downs. A regular in the Downs stable area during Derby Week, Price stops to shake hands with racing people and reminisce about the old days. The ever-popular Price is frequently interviewed by writers and television people. And all because of Carry Back.

Following the 1994 Derby, the eighty-six-year-old Price said that if it hadn't been for Carry Back "I would have been just a statistic."

As it is, Price is walking proof that winning the Kentucky Derby is an honor you carry with you the rest of your life. "I can go to any racetrack in the country and be walking through the grandstand or the clubhouse," Price said, "and you can hear, 'There's Jack Price. He had the 1961 Derby winner.'"

Carry Back was more than just a Derby winner. He was "the people's choice," a colt whom fans flocked to the racetrack to see. People's moods, not just their money, were affected by the outcome of races involving Carry Back. His appeal stretched beyond the track itself, and it seemed that even the man on the street had heard of his racing exploits. In 1961, the year that he was a champion, Carry Back ran sixteen times at eight different tracks in front of crowds totaling 533,325.

He holds the distinction of being the most durable Derby winner in modern times. Since 1921, only one Derby winner—Whiskery, the 1927 victor who finished his career with seventy races to his credit—ran more times than Carry Back's sixty-one starts.

Carry Back had a fierce rivalry during his career with Crozier. The two horses met ten times, and Carry Back finished ahead of Crozier in seven of those races.

Although Crozier would be called a "bridesmaid," losing to Carry Back was no disgrace. The electrifying Carry Back was a remarkable horse. He faced the toughest competition available, he carried heavy weights, he won distance races, and he set track records.

Price could have handled Carry Back conservatively and

spotted him in lesser races that he would most likely have won with no trouble. But Price, ever the sportsman, had a champion in his barn, and he repeatedly ran Carry Back against the best.

Carry Back raced against such American champions as five-time Horse of the Year Kelso, Mongo, T. V. Lark, Never Bend, Hail to Reason, Ridan, Crimson Satan, and Intentionally, as well as foreign stars Match II, Val de Loir, Monade, Soltikoff, Aurelius, Exbury, and Zabeg.

A freight train on legs, Carry Back carried a total of 7,462 pounds during his career, winning once each with such burdens as 130 and 133 pounds.

Carry Back's sixty-one career races covered a total of 62 miles, ranging from three furlongs to a mile and five-eighths. He won a dozen races longer than a mile, including four at a mile and a quarter. He set two track records, one sprinting five furlongs ($57\frac{3}{5}$ at Gulfstream Park, 1960) and the other at the classic $1\frac{1}{4}$-mile distance (2:00$\frac{2}{5}$ at Monmouth Park, 1962). He equaled another track record at a mile (Aqueduct), a distance at which he won five races.

Track surfaces didn't matter. He won on three sloppy tracks and two muddy surfaces. He also won one race on the grass.

Carry Back and his camp traveled all over. He appeared at fifteen tracks and ran in eight states. He also crossed the Atlantic for a race.

He won by as little as a head, as much as 8 lengths. He was favored in thirty-four races, fifteen of which resulted in victories. He was ridden by eleven different jockeys. John Sellers, his jockey in the Triple Crown races, was aboard him for twenty-five starts, winning thirteen.

In 1962, Carry Back was sent to France, the first Kentucky Derby winner to race in the Prix de l'Arc de Triomphe. He finished tenth among twenty-four starters, but he was beaten by only $5\frac{3}{4}$ lengths by the victorious Soltikoff after receiving an unsatisfactory ride from forty-eight-year-old Australian Scobie Breasley. "We lost through a combination of bad racing luck and a stupid ride," Price said a day after the race.

Carry Back won twenty-one races, including fourteen that were added-money affairs. His last triumph, in the 1963 Trenton Handicap, provided Price with an especially big kick.

Carry Back, who originally had been "retired" after his 1962 campaign, stood his first season at stud in Florida in 1963. Later in 1963, however, he was brought back to the races. Price was criticized by some for racing Carry Back beyond his peak and was under tremendous pressure to retire the horse. But as so often was the case with Carry Back's racing career, Price was right.

The Trenton was Carry Back's first start since he ran next-to-last 3½ weeks earlier in the Manhattan Handicap, beaten by 16 lengths.

The critics "thought there was something wrong with the horse and I was hungry to get the money or something like that," said Price. "I had taken so much criticism. People were writing me letters. I knew there was nothing wrong with the horse, and I wanted to prove it to them."

Carry Back won the Trenton by 2½ lengths over Mongo on a muddy track. "I did something that very few people had done before—brought a horse back from the stud and then wind up winning a stake with him in his final race," said Price. "Then I said, 'Now I'm really going to retire him.'"

Even after he was retired for good, Carry Back showed off his old spark on a special occasion in New York. In 1966, three years after Carry Back's last race, Price went to the trouble—and took the risk—of sending the horse from Kentucky to Aqueduct for an appearance at an "Old Timers Day" celebration. Carry Back was no stranger to the Big Apple. He had raced nineteen times in New York City. Indeed, he started more times at Aqueduct (thirteen) than he did at any other track.

Carry Back was greeted with cheers on this nostalgic afternoon. The horses on display were expected to do nothing more than go onto the track and walk or lope the length of the grandstand. Carry Back didn't want anything to do with this leisurely business. With the crowd roaring its approval, he took off running.

Pinky Hurley, a veteran exercise rider who was aboard Carry Back, couldn't hold the horse, said Price. "He was supposed to pull up at the winner's circle and he couldn't hold him and I kept waving him on. He didn't get him pulled up until he was way on the backside. And then he never did come back. He just went on back to the barn."

Carry Back's sensational stretch runs, coupled with his rags-to-riches background, caught the fancy of the racing public. Unlike all too many racehorses, he wasn't here today and gone tomorrow. He raced for four seasons, enough time to make an everlasting impression. "It's hard for people to forget a horse that's been in the limelight that many years in a row," said Price. "I think that's one of the reasons for his popularity."

Carry Back received fan mail for years. His most devoted follower was Marianne Hight of Glenview, Ill. She wouldn't write directly to the Prices. She'd address her mail to Carry Back himself, sending him Christmas and Easter cards. In 1970, she went to Florida and delivered a blanket to Carry Back. In 1974, she mailed a blanket to him. "I still sent cards and later on sent apples to him at Christmas and a large latch-hook stocking for Christmas," Hight wrote in 1983. "In 1980, my husband and I went to Florida on vacation, and it was another opportunity to see Carry Back. It was near Halloween, so we bought a Trick or Treat shopping bag and filled it with bags of marshmallows. I knew Carry Back loved them. Mr. Price let us feed some of them to Carry Back."

Carry Back was retired from breeding after the 1982 season. At stud, he was represented by some hard-knocking horses, including Sharp Gary, who amassed a bankroll of $535,198 from 115 starts. Sharp Gary was foaled on May 5, 1971, one day before the tenth anniversary of his father's Derby victory.

It's too bad Carry Back didn't sire more like Sharp Gary.

"Carry Back was just an average stallion, but he got worse-than-average mares," said Price. "I was my own worst enemy there. In the first place, I took any mare that came along, instead of being selective. Of course, I was green. I wasn't a breeder, I was a trainer."

Price always had a special place in his heart for Carry Back. After he was informed of Carry Back's 1975 election to the Hall of Fame, Price paid the horse a visit. "I got a piece of sugar and took it to him," he said. "I gave him the sugar, then sat down there at the stall for ten or fifteen minutes and talked to him. By the time we'd finished our recollections, I was crying a little, I think, but Carry Back seemed awfully proud."

Carry Back was so named "because we had a few years of losses in the horse business and we hoped this colt would win enough so that we could carry back those profits to the loss years," explained Price.

Price added that Matt Reddy, the groom for Carry Back, had another version of how the horse was named. "He claimed that Mrs. Price named him that because I had to be carried back home after a few drinks."

As a youngster, Carry Back was nicknamed "Blackie." "But then when he got famous we called him C. B.," said Price, laughing.

Carry Back handled old age quite well. He had the physical appearance of a younger horse. "He is not swayback, and he does not show his age," Price said in early 1983. "He looks beautiful. The horse looks like he's fifteen."

The Prices, parents of two daughters, considered Carry Back a member of the family, too. Price liked to refer to the horse as "our son, the stallion, Carry Back."

The Prices' "son" died in 1983. A malignant tumor had spread, and surgery revealed there was no hope for him and that he would always be in pain. The Prices loved Carry Back too much to have him suffer, so the twenty-five-year-old horse was put to sleep on March 24, 1983. His body was cremated. Price picked up Carry Back's remains, which were in a box.

"I was walking down the stairs out of the lobby to get to my car, and I was talking to him, just like I always did when he was living," Jack Price said. "And I said, 'Son, you carried me for a long ways. Now I'm carrying you.'"

Katherine was walking alongside Jack. "She was crying," he said. "So was I."

Carry Back's remains first were buried in Florida before being reinterred in ol' Kentucky.

Katherine Price died on February 14, 1987. She and Jack had been married fifty-five years. Fighting cancer, she attended her last Derby in 1986. Despite her sickness, she wasn't one to put a damper on things. Instead, just a few hours after the 1986 Derby, she and Jack, along with another couple, were enjoying a drink in the Executive Inn in Louisville when this wonderful woman suddenly raised her glass and proposed a toast. She said: "Here's to the 1987 Kentucky Derby," a race that she would not live to see.

She commented that evening about how happy she was that Carry Back was buried on the grounds of the Kentucky Derby Museum. The remains are in the museum's garden, not too far from the Churchill Downs homestretch, where in 1961 Carry Back made up more than 13 lengths in the final quarter of a mile to win the Run for the Roses.

5

Whatever Happened to Holy Land?

IT MUST BE IN THE GENES—the Bolus genes, that is. Throughout the long history of the Kentucky Derby, 1,457 horses have started, and only two have lost their jockeys during the running of the race. In 1936, Granville unseated his jockey, Jimmy Stout, coming out of the starting gate. My dad, Eli, wagered on Granville that day. Thirty-four years later, in 1970, Holy Land stumbled and fell near the five-sixteenths pole in the Derby, losing his jockey, Hector Pilar. Yours truly wagered on Holy Land that day.

I predict that in the year 2004 another starter will lose his jockey in the Derby—and that my son, Bo, or daughter, Jennifer, will wager on that particular horse.

This thing about picking horses who lose their jockeys isn't restricted to the Derby. In the 1974 Preakness, Buck's Bid stumbled his first stride away from the starting gate and unseated his jockey, Don MacBeth. Looking on in amazement from the Pimlico press box was this writer, who had wagered on Buck's Bid, a horse I had been touted on in the Derby by none other than my father.

With my family having a knack for picking jockeys unseated in Triple Crown races, you can fully appreciate why I

Holy Land, with Hector Pilar up, is shown in the winner's circle following his victory in a maiden race on March 6, 1970 at Gulfstream Park. (Courtesy Raftery-Turfotos)

have given up ever trying to pick the winner of one of these races. All I ask is that my horse finish the race with his jockey in the same position he was in at the start—on the creature's back. That, to me, is a moral victory.

Forty years after Granville unseated Stout, I was interviewing the former jockey by telephone and I mentioned to him that my father had wagered on his horse in the Derby. I sent Stout a photograph of Granville unseating him coming out of the gate, and he was kind enough to autograph it for my father, writing that he was sorry that Eli had lost his bet in that race.

As for Holy Land, I was ribbed and kidded for quite a few years after the 1970 Derby.

"Hey, Bolus, you bum! Whatever happened to Holy Land?"

"Hey, world's great handicapper, do you still have your Holy Land tickets?"

"Holy Land? Bolus, you couldn't pick Whirlaway out of a herd of buffalo."

Some people will *never* let you forget.

But in all seriousness, I believed then, as I do now, that if Holy Land had experienced a smooth trip in the Derby, he would have been right there at the finish. But we'll never know.

Late Foal Began Blossoming at Three

Holy Land, a late foal who was born May 29, 1967, started twice as a two-year-old, finishing fifth at Saratoga and second at Belmont Park. Jean Cruguet rode him in both maiden races.

At three, Holy land won all three of his starts before the Derby—each at a mile and one-sixteenth at Gulfstream Park. Hector Pilar rode him in the three races.

"My Horse Can Run All Day"

When newsmen converged on Churchill Downs in the morning hours leading up to the 1970 Run for the Roses, they automatically headed to Barns 41 and 42, where the majority of the Derby horses were in residence.

That was fine with trainer Jack Weipert. He had a horse stabled down the way in Barn 37, and he was glad that his runner was away from the spotlight of photographers and reporters. His horse was Holy Land.

"I got news for you," Weipert said six days before the Derby as he hosed cold water on Holy Land's forelegs. "I wouldn't be here if I didn't think I could win the Derby."

Weipert could understand clearly why Holy Land was being overlooked by the news media. "The publicity always goes to the stakes winners," he said. "This horse is going to have to prove himself. I think he can do it, but he's got to show everybody else."

The only horse of note whom Holy Land had beaten was Cassie Red, who finished second in an April 15 race, losing by 2 lengths.

Weipert had planned on running Holy Land in the Florida Derby, but the colt was knocked out of training with a nasal problem. "It happened about five days before the Florida Derby," the heavyset trainer explained. "Horses all over the racetrack had it. It put us back at least two weeks in training. I wish the Derby was another week away. We'd really be ready for it then."

Weipert, a training veteran of twenty-four years, purchased Holy Land for $15,000 on behalf of J. Simpson Dean, Jr., at Keeneland's 1968 fall yearling sale. Bred by A. B. Karsner in Kentucky, the colt was by Promised Land out of Duchess Brown, by Solar Slipper. Holy Land raced in the name of Mrs. Dean, of Wilmington, Del.

"I haven't rushed him," said Weipert. "I told the owner last year we'd only break him down trying for all those two-year-old races. I thought this was a Derby horse ever since I've had him, and I knew he'd be suited for the longer races when he's three and four. His best races are ahead of him. I have to give him a chance to run in the Derby to see what he can do."

Most trainers were hoping that their runners drew advantageous post positions in the expected large field, but Holy Land's starting spot didn't concern Weipert in the least."I'm not going to go for the lead anyway," he said. "I'm going to run when it counts—in the stretch. The hell with that first turn. Let 'em all go tearing into it. Not me. These other Derby horses, some of them are nothing more than sprinters and they're trying to make 'em run a mile and a quarter. My horse can run all day. I know that for a fact."

Holy Land was not particularly impressive in appearance. The chestnut colt was tall and lean, not at all muscular. "He's not much to look at," Weipert admitted, "but they're not running a beauty contest this Saturday afternoon."

On Monday morning of Derby Week, Holy Land put in his final major workout, going a mile in 1:39⅖. "A mile in :39 for him is like :37 for any other horse," Weipert said. "He's just not a good work horse."

Holy Land entered the Derby with paltry earnings of $12,025, the lowest in the field. His five career races were the fewest among the seventeen Derby starters. He drew post position No. 4 and was listed at 15-1 in the program's morning line.

In its poll of sportswriters and sportscasters covering the Derby, *The Courier-Journal* reported that My Dad George was picked to win by 31 journalists, Personality by 20, Silent Screen and Dr. Behrman by 11 each, Corn Off the Cob by 10, Holy Land by 9—"and the others were equally divided."

"Thunder Struck" in the Downs Stable Area

On Derby Eve, a headline over an Andrew Beyer column in *The Washington (N.C.) Daily News* provided the following tip: *Make it Holy Land.*

Beyer wrote that he came to Louisville with a two-rule system for picking the Derby winner. Rule No. 1—"If an owner, trainer or jockey has been making excuses for his horse, eliminate the horse." Rule No. 2—"If there is any doubt that a colt will relish running a mile and a quarter, eliminate him."

Beyer wrote that the two rules eliminated all but two horses—My Dad George and Holy Land.

"We weren't totally convinced by these conclusions until meeting a brother system-maker on the Churchill Downs backstretch," Beyer wrote. "He was a Louisville writer named Jim Bolus, and he said he had done extensive research into Derby history to create a sure-fire system.

"According to his method one considers only horses which (1) finished first or second in their last two races; (2) ran farther than a mile in one of those races; (3) prepared for the Derby at major tracks; and (4) have won half of their races as a 3-year-old.

"This year, Bolus said, three horses qualify. One is Terlago, but Bolus didn't like Terlago—which, after all, is a system inventor's prerogative.

"Bolus said the other two horses who qualify—thunder

struck as he spoke the words—are Holy Land and My Dad George."

Beyer concluded his column with this observation: "Until tomorrow afternoon, there will be no way to tell if Holy Land has class. But, at least, all the other Derby entrants have had ample opportunity to demonstrate that they are not exceptional. Holy Land is still untested, but if there is a first rate thorobred in this Kentucky Derby, he is the one. At 15 to 1 we bet that he is."

Where *Was* Holy Land?

I watched the Derby from a perfect viewing spot on the outside of the Churchill Downs press box. Rancho Lejos, a speedball, led the way the first time past the wire and on down the backstretch. Holy Land, who had gone off at 15.90-1, was far back, but there was no reason to worry at this point. He was expected to deliver his kick in the homestretch. As the field reached the far turn, track announcer Chic Anderson said: "They're very well bunched as they move into that turn."

I never did see Holy Land go down.

While little Dust Commander charged through the stretch to win by 5 lengths, I quickly scanned the rest of the field for Holy Land, fully expecting him to be in the first flight of horses. He wasn't. I never did see him cross the wire. With no reason to think that Holy Land had been involved in a mishap, I figured that he was back in the pack somewhere and I just missed him as he came through the stretch. Little did I know.

In his call of the race, Anderson didn't mention the incident, and I don't believe that many writers spotted the trouble during the running of the race.

Shortly after the race was over, I went inside the press box and noticed some of the newsmen looking at a television monitor. Something had happened near the five-sixteenths pole, and this incident was being shown. It was then that I learned what had happened to Holy Land.

I later was told that the riderless horse ran down the stretch near the outside rail, coming close to some journalists standing on the track.

At first, it was reported by many, including this writer, that Holy Land had stumbled, but he did more than that—he actually fell to the ground, as *Daily Racing Form* chart caller Bud Lyon pointed out in the footnotes of the Derby's chart. Leo O'Donnell, one of the stewards, said Holy Land "just took a bad step, stumbled and fell." The colt fell "just enough to take the boy off."

Pilar, it was originally reported, fractured his first lumbar vertebra. (He later would say he suffered fractures of several lumbar vertebrae.) Doctors estimated that Pilar would not be able to resume riding for six months to a year.

Mike Venezia finished thirteenth aboard Action Getter in that Derby and afterward said: "All I was looking for was a hole along the fence—for room just like everybody else. I went right over his [Pilar's] horse's rump." (Venezia avoided the accident with Holy Land, but eighteen years later he would be killed in a spill at Belmont Park.)

Admiral's Shield, who finished sixth in the Derby, was directly in back of Holy Land at the time of the accident and somehow managed to avoid the fallen horse and jockey. Jimmy Nichols, who rode Admiral's Shield, later said: "Holy Land went to his knees, and he got up in a hurry. If he had gone down and turned over, four or five of us could have been in a bad spill. Somebody could have been hurt real seriously, a lot worse than what happened to Pilar. As it was, my horse jumped to miss the jockey. He was running real handily before that happened. We were close to Broussard [Ray Broussard, aboard eventual runner-up My Dad George], and he was humping away on his horse. I was just sitting there on my horse. I had a handful of horse under me.

"Then that jockey went down, and my horse had to jump to the side. My horse jumped four or five feet high over that jockey that went down. Oh, what a jam. I knew somebody had to go down. We lost a lot of ground. We passed some horses in the stretch, but my horse never really did get back on stride. I think he would have finished second or third if the jockey hadn't gone down. After that incident, he just wasn't able to come up with a kick—like he had in the Trial."

In the Derby Trial, Admiral's Shield came from behind over a sloppy track to score a 1-length victory. He paid $42 to win. At 29-1 odds in the Derby, Admiral's Shield was the longest price on the board.

Harvey Vanier, the trainer of Admiral's Shield, years later recalled: "Good thing Jimmy was an old cowboy. He did a good job keeping the horse up on his feet. He jumped over that horse, and he still finished sixth. I always thought I had a Derby winner there if he hadn't met a problem like that."

Vanier said Admiral's Shield suffered an injury in that Derby. "He kind of sprained his shoulder," the trainer said. "He was never quite the same horse after that."

Neither was Holy Land.

"I Yelled When I Saw My Colors in a Heap"

The morning after the 1970 Derby, I naturally headed to Holy Land's barn to check on the colt. Mrs. Dean, the colt's owner, was there, and she said she was the first person in her clubhouse box to know that her horse had thrown Pilar. "I yelled when I saw my pink and green colors in a heap on the side of the racetrack," she said. "Nobody around me knew what happened. I didn't see Holy Land run up against anybody or bump another horse, but I did see the colors in a pile on the track."

In a later interview, Mrs. Dean said: "I couldn't believe my eyes. Holy Land just went out of sight. All I saw was jockey Hector Pilar come flying out of the saddle."

It was reported the day after the '70 Derby that Holy Land had come out of the race with a few cuts and fluid in the main joint of his left hind leg. "He's all right this morning," said Weipert, "but he didn't eat last night after the race. We really won't know how bad he's hurt for a couple of days."

Weipert wasn't sure how Holy Land lost his bridle and blinkers in the incident. "When Pilar went off, he could have pulled them off," the trainer opined. "The horse could have done it himself. He could have ripped everything off. I couldn't see it myself. Pilar went down behind all those people in the infield."

Weipert had said before the race that Holy Land would do his running in the homestretch, but the colt never had a chance to do so. He was moving well—and then he fell. As Mrs. Dean said, "We were just where we wanted to be. We were ready to make our move then. Now we'll never know what would have happened.

"Everybody seemed to think it was My Dad George we ran up against," she added.

"In the Derby, you take chances," Weipert said. "Pilar thought it was time to go with the horse—and he couldn't make it through. That's all.

"I'll tell you one thing, though. I'll never run another Derby horse in a field of seventeen unless my horse can lay first, second, or third. No more come-from-behind horses for me in a field that big."

As it would turn out, Weipert would never run another horse in the Derby.

Never Fulfilled His Potential

As far as I was concerned, the Holy Land story continued to live following the 1970 Derby. I was interested in the horse, his jockey, and his trainer.

Holy Land never was able to live up to his full potential following his Derby mishap. He made his comeback on April 9, 1971 at Gulfstream Park, finishing eighth in a turf race. He then ran third in four straight races before winning a 1$\frac{1}{16}$-mile grass race as the even-money favorite June 3 at Delaware Park. Pilar was aboard the colt in that 2¼-length victory.

In the *Daily Racing Form* of June 12, 1971, William C.

Phillips wrote: "Holy Land appeared so physically drawn and incapacitated when the writer saw him turned out last summer that we frankly would not have given a plug nickel for his chances to resume a racing career."

Said Weipert: "It was awfully sad to look at him, but I never doubted he would make it because I knew he had the class and the determination. It was his hock that was injured when he fell in the Derby. It wasn't until I tried training him early last winter in Florida that I discovered he had a broken ankle in front, too. It probably happened at the same time. I don't suppose we'll ever know how good he might have been if it hadn't been for his injuries. But, even so, he's pretty good."

On July 5, 1971, Holy Land won again with Pilar up in a one-mile grass race at Delaware. Tryandstopme, the favorite, was second, and Barbizon Streak ran third.

Holy Land didn't race again that year but returned to competition April 22, 1972, at Hialeah Park. He then was out of action until August 15 at Saratoga, and on that day in a *Daily Racing Form* story written by Teddy Cox, Weipert was quoted as saying: "I've had my share of bad-luck horses with unsound underpinning, but I think Holy Land is the most remarkable horse I've ever been around on this score. He has more guts and determination than you can believe."

Of Holy Land's comeback, Weipert said: "It was a long, tough fight for the colt, but he overcame these ailments and we finally got him back to the races. Naturally, it took some time for him to regain his poise and confidence."

Defeated Canonero II

In seven starts as a five-year-old, Holy Land won once, but that one victory fully demonstrated this horse's capabilities against top competition. On September 1, 1972, with Laffit Pincay, Jr., in the saddle, Holy Land captured a 1$\frac{1}{16}$-mile allowance at Belmont Park, defeating Naskra (who finished fourth) and 1971 Derby winner Canonero II (fifth).

Dollars and Donuts

On February 11, 1973, Holy Land won a mile-and-forty-yard allowance at the Fair Grounds in New Orleans. A week later at the same track, he ran second, again going a mile and forty yards. Then six days later, he captured his first (and only) stakes race, the 1⅛-mile Letellier Memorial Handicap, in sloppy going. List, the 1.30-1 favorite, ran second, losing by a half-length.

Following the Letellier, Weipert said: "He's beaten lots of stakes horses. It's time he won one of his own."

Recalling the 1970 Derby accident, Weipert said of Holy Land: "He came out of it with a broken ankle. That was the start of his problems, and believe me there have been many of them." Indeed, Holy Land reportedly was dead lame five days before the Letellier "and he cooled out none too well after the race."

Weipert said Holy Land "could hardly walk last week" and that during the February 18 race he sustained a quarter crack, making the foot sore all week. "The rain helped out. He likes a soft track, as you might expect."

Writing in the *Daily Racing Form,* Dan Kenny noted: "The Deans left for a night on the town. Before heading out into the downpour, Mrs. Dean asked a native the whereabouts of the nearest donut shop. 'For Holy Land, of course. His favorite food is jelly donuts. Eats as many as you'll give him.'

"The horse deserves them. The dollars and the donuts."

Holy Land started six more times, losing each race. His last four races produced three straight fourth-place finishes, followed by a third in his career finale.

The bottom line on Holy Land was that he won three of five starts before the 1970 Derby and five of twenty-four afterward. He added two seconds and six thirds to his eight victories, giving him sixteen in-the-money finishes. He earned $68,185.

One of his victories was at a mile, the other seven at longer distances. He may very well have been the best distance horse in that 1970 Derby.

The Words I Wanted to Hear

In the fall of 1976, Pilar returned to Churchill Downs to ride, and I didn't waste any time interviewing him. On the first day of the meeting, I went to the jockeys' room. The next day, a story of mine in *The Louisville Times* led off in this fashion:

"When last seen at Churchill Downs, jockey Hector Pilar was hurting. Literally.

"Grimacing in pain, he was being placed on a stretcher to be whisked away in an ambulance to a hospital.

"It was Derby Day, 1970, an afternoon that Pilar will never forget. He was injured in a spill during the running of the 96th Kentucky Derby as a result of being unseated from his mount, Holy Land, who fell about midway on the turn for home.

"Pilar suffered fractures of several lumbar vertebrae in the accident.

"The jockey subsequently made a comeback but until this fall, when he rode at Keeneland, he hadn't returned to Kentucky to ply his trade. And now he is back competing at Churchill Downs, back at the scene of the accident that was one of the most spectacular incidents in the history of the Derby."

During the interview, the thirty-eight-year-old Pilar told me he had been on the Maryland circuit for the most part since he had last ridden at Churchill Downs. I asked him what had brought him back to Kentucky. "I've been riding for trainer Mike Tinker," he said, "and he asked me if I wanted to ride some horses for him in Kentucky. He has some nice horses and I no have too much to ride in Maryland so I said I might as well take a trip down here. And, so far, I haven't been doing too bad, you know."

Pilar, a native of Chile, had begun his career in South

America. He first started riding in the United States in 1966, the year that he won his only Churchill Downs stakes—the Clark Handicap.

In recalling his accident in the Derby, Pilar said his mount clipped the heels of Terlago. "Holy Land went down," he said. "He completely roll over."

Pilar then told me what I had gone to the jockeys' room to hear him say. He said he believed that Holy Land would have won the Derby if he hadn't gone down.

"He was one of the best horses I ever rode around here in the United States," he said. "He won couple of allowances in Florida, and he won in a nice way. And when we work him here a distance, he worked really good and I have a lot of horse, so I say, 'This horse is gonna run big in the race.'"

Most jockeys never get a chance to ride in the Derby, and, for Pilar, the 1970 running would be his only appearance in the race. He gave it his best shot—and maybe, as the field bunched up on the final turn, he took a shot that he shouldn't have. "Everybody wants to win big races, so they no give you too much shot and everybody takes a chance, too," he said. "And I think I take a chance that day, and it was bad luck, that's all."

Holy Land was moving extremely well when the accident happened. "That's why I think he could win the race because I never asked him before and when I started to ask him, he started just movin'," Pilar said.

But before he could get rolling into high gear, Holy Land went down, throwing Pilar.

Ironically, the very first ride that Pilar made on his comeback trail occurred on Derby Day, 1971, at Garden State Park. And he won. Appropriately, he rode the winner, a colt named Shadyside, for Mrs. Dean and Weipert, the same owner and trainer of Holy Land.

"I rode Holy Land when he came back [in 1971]," Pilar said. "Win a couple of races with him. But he never was the same horse I rode before [the 1970 Derby] because in the spill he broke some bone and he never was the same horse."

With a grin, Pilar added: "But he still was game, anyway."

Pilar no doubt has long forgotten my interview with him, but I never have. Later, on a trip to the Preakness one year, I saw Pilar in the Pimlico jockeys' room, and I asked him to autograph my program. He obliged.

Hector Pilar . . . one of my Derby heroes.

More Bad Luck for Weipert at the Downs

On opening day of the 1980 fall meeting at Churchill Downs, Weipert ran Miss Swing Time, a two-year-old filly, in the featured race. I went to the paddock before the race to shake hands with Weipert and remind him of my allegiance to Holy Land. I asked the veteran trainer if he had returned to Churchill Downs previously to saddle a horse since the 1970 Derby. He said he had—once.

Then something incredibly eerie happened in the race. Weipert witnessed a replay of his nightmare in the 1970 Derby.

On a gloomy afternoon, Weipert sent out Miss Swing Time in the eighth race, a six-furlong allowance run on a track rated as good. Unlike Holy Land, she didn't come back.

On the turn for home, the same turn where Holy Land went down in 1970, Miss Swing Time did the same thing. But her mishap was worse than Holy Land's. She suffered a broken leg and had to be destroyed. Her jockey, Julio Espinoza, wasn't injured.

As soon as the race was over, I hurriedly found Weipert. "Damn racetrack's bad luck for me," he said.

Walking through the paddock tunnel leading to the track, he didn't know how seriously his filly had been injured.

"You better go down there and see what's going on, Willie," Weipert told a groom, who promptly hustled up the track to where Miss Swing Time was lying.

A man came up to Weipert and said: "Snapped it off just like that, Jack."

"Broken leg?" Weipert inquired.

"Yeah, I was looking through the binoculars."

Weipert then began to walk up the track to take a look at his filly.

"I hope that jock didn't get hurt," he said, trudging through the mud near the outer railing.

Weipert couldn't yet see Miss Swing Time, who had gone down between the five-sixteenths pole and the quarter pole, just before the field had straightened out for the homestretch. But far off in the distance the track's ambulance's lights could be seen blinking.

"She looked like she was moving up to the lead, didn't she?" Weipert said.

While Weipert was walking to his filly, the ambulance was coming down the stretch with Espinoza. Noticing the jockey, Weipert said: "He's all right, the jock. He's sitting up."

Mention was made of Holy Land's accident. "He chipped his hock and ankle," recalled Weipert.

Weipert had high hopes for Miss Swing Time and had looked forward to racing her in the Pocahontas Stakes on Thanksgiving Day at the Downs. "Nice filly," said Weipert. "Sound as a dollar."

Making his way up the track, now slightly more than a sixteenth of a mile from Miss Swing Time, Weipert spotted her lying on her side. "She's dead," he said. "Jock's lucky he didn't get hurt."

But Miss Swing Time wasn't dead—not just yet, anyway. She rolled over on her other side.

Shortly, track veterinarian Nicholas Salvatore injected Miss Swing Time, and she was dead in a matter of seconds.

Later, Salvatore would describe the procedure: "Medical euthanasia administered by a syringe. It's extremely rapid and humane and painless. There was no chance for her. We made sure we had permission."

The day was misty and gray—and, for the feature, the track was "off," officially listed as good. Weipert questioned the wisdom of racing a horse in such going. "Running a horse in the mud, you got to be insane," he said.

Back at the clubhouse, Weipert was offered sympathy. "Tough luck, Jack," somebody said to him.

"Yeah," Weipert replied with a shrug.

Years later, Weipert would recall the incident with Miss Swing Time and say: "She was back in the knees—and that one knee, in particular. When they run in the mud, when they got a fault, it'll come out in them. I should never have run her that day."

Jack Weipert, the trainer of Holy Land. (Courtesy Raftery-Turfotos)

Weipert Asked Just One Favor

In 1990, two decades after Holy Land's Derby, I saw Weipert at Gulfstream Park and made it a point to shake hands with the veteran trainer. I told him that my father had picked Granville and that I had selected Holy Land, the only two horses in Derby history to lose their jockeys.

Weipert smiled and said, "I probably will never get back to the Derby, but if I do, please do me a favor and *don't* pick my horse."

What *Did* Ever Happen to Holy Land?

Mrs. Dean, in whose name Holy Land raced, died in 1989.

In 1993, we placed a call to Mr. Dean, who attended the 1970 Derby with his wife.

Recalling the Derby, Dean said of Holy Land: "He had been training real well. He was 15-1, and Dust Commander was also 15-1. We expected Holy Land to run well. There wasn't any great standout in the Derby that year. The only thing wrong was just a very large field.

"Holy Land was a very nice, honest horse. He was fun to own. Of course, when he got hurt at the Derby, he did recover, but he never was as good as he was."

In recent years, we also talked with Weipert about Holy Land. Weipert, retired from training, said he didn't think Holy Land came back 100 percent from his Derby injuries. "He come back and ran real good," Weipert said, "but I think he was better before. He was never the same horse. He was always getting quarter cracks after the Derby and he never did that before. I don't know why that happened, but that's why he only run a few times every year. He'd always come up with a quarter crack."

During Holy Land's days at stud, Dean wound up giving the stallion to Weipert.

Weipert himself later gave Holy Land away. "I sent him to South America to be a stud down there," he said. "I gave him to the man that run that racetrack in Peru. Something happened with him down there. I never did find out, but he died. Sometimes them old studs—I don't know what he was, about thirteen or fourteen then—when you send them to another place, they do that; they don't live very long. I don't know why it is."

In the case of Holy Land, an accident might have been the cause of his death. "I never could get from them people what really happened," Weipert said. "It sounded like he fell over backwards. Maybe he had a shank over his nose—he was a tough horse to handle, you know—and he might have got a little rank and they snatched him and he fell over backwards and hit his head. It killed him, that's all. I don't know that for sure, but that's what I surmised from what they were telling me.

"I thought I was doing the right thing for the horse, sending him down there," Weipert added. "He would have got forty, fifty mares [a season]. I just wanted him to get a good home.

Looking back on that 1970 Derby, Weipert said: "I thought he had a good chance. That was a bad year for the Derby."

Asked what he thinks would have happened in the race if Holy Land hadn't fallen, Weipert replied: "I don't know. All I can tell you is the rider told me later on that the horse was moving real good and he hadn't asked him to run yet. And he thought he had a good chance of winning.

"But that'll never be proved," Weipert added, chuckling.

In another interview, Weipert expressed this opinion of how Holy Land would have fared in that Derby had he not fallen: "He'da been right there, there's no doubt about it. Maybe he wouldn't have beat the winner. The winner run big that day, the race of his life. But he would have beat the rest of them.

"How do you know? You're guessing, that's all. But I know he would have been right there, that's for sure.

"He wasn't no great horse, but he was a damn good horse, an honest horse. He was a superior mudder. He could beat anybody in the mud. He should have won a lot more stakes."

Would Holy Land Have Won That '70 Derby?

Not only did Holy Land have bad luck as a horse running in the Derby, but when it came to this race he had bad luck as a sire. To Holy Land's misfortune, the only Derby starter he ever sired was Great Redeemer. Holy Land deserved better than that. Great Redeemer, an overmatched colt who should never have run in the Derby, came in last in the 1979 renewal.

But at least he finished the race. Holy Land didn't have a chance to finish what he had set out to do—that is, to try to win the roses.

We'll never know whether Holy Land would have won the 1970 Derby, but one thing that we all *should* know is that he wouldn't have finished last. Yet, because he fell in the Derby, his name appears in the chart under that of Rancho Lejos, who led in the early going before retreating and bringing up the rear among the actual finishers.

There are "Unofficial Cups" listing the Derby's last-place finishers, and Holy Land's name appears next to the year 1970. To suggest that this colt finished last in his Derby is misleading and a falsehood. Besides that, it irritates me.

How could anybody say that Holy Land finished last in his Derby? He never finished the race. And if he *had* finished the race, he wouldn't have been last. He was moving impressively at the time of his accident, preparing to do his running in the long Churchill Downs stretch.

Holy Land a last-place finisher? You gotta be kidding. There's no doubt in my mind he would have been a strong finisher in that Derby—maybe even the winner.

Herb Stevens held Rockhill Native, with Johnny Oldham up. Rockhill Native finished fifth as the favorite in the 1980 Kentucky Derby. (Courtesy Keeneland Association)

6

That Stevens Family: True Hardboots

FOR A LONG TIME—indeed, for more than 120 years—there has been at least one member of the Stevens family participating in horse racing.

The Kentucky family's racing roots go back to John Stevens, who traded horses and raced them, too. John's horses were trained by his son, Thomas H., who was quite successful for many years. Next there was Thomas H.'s son, James, a highly respected trainer himself. And following in the family tradition were two of James' sons, fourth-generation horsemen Herb and Thomas H. Stevens, Sr. The latter, usually called Tommy, also had a son, Thomas H. ("Tee") Stevens, Jr., who himself has trained horses.

The Stevens family originally engaged in the horse-trading business about the time of the Civil War. In their horse-trading activities, the Stevens men eventually wound up with a Thoroughbred—and that's how they got started racing that particular breed.

Back in the nineteenth century, John Stevens and his son, Thomas H., had a foolproof method of winning with another breed—quarter horses. They would journey from town to town by buggy, a quarter horse pulling the rig while another such horse, loping along at an easy clip, would be tied to the back. Just before they would arrive in town, they'd switch horses, hooking up the fresh one to the buggy.

Upon their arrival in town, the conversation naturally would get around to horses. In those days, there was inevitably one guy in every town with the local favorite, the fastest riding horse in those parts. Next thing you'd know, the horse talk would develop into an argument and John Stevens would get around to declaring, "Hell, I got a buggy horse that can beat *that* horse."

The townspeople, properly insulted and thinking that the Stevens horse had been tired out by pulling the buggy, promptly whipped their money out—and the betting was on.

Once the race was on, the Stevens runner sped along like the fresh horse that he was. Thomas H., a little man, would ride the horse, and, according to the story handed down through the years, the Stevens horsemen never lost a bet in one of those match races.

Thomas H. Stevens was one of the most successful horsemen in the country during his time. Stevens, whose forte with Thoroughbreds was said to be training long-distance runners, died in 1912 at the age of sixty. "Mr. Stevens was a horseman from his birth and began his career as a racing man by racing quarter horses for his father on the banks of the Kentucky River," reported *The Thoroughbred Record.* "The order of the game was 'touch and go and every fellow take care of himself,' but it was always on the up and up. Stevens knew it thoroughly, and there was none better at it in his day. His aptitude at quarter racing was the foundation of a comfortable competence, out of which he lived well until his death. He had an enduring reputation for fair dealing on and off the turf."

He won numerous stakes, including the 1887 Kentucky Oaks when two of his fillies, Florimore and Wary, finished first and second. Wary was favored, but the stable won the race (and no doubt some bets) with Florimore, who was third choice.

The Courier-Journal's account of the race read, in part,

"This was the Kentucky Oaks, distance one and one-half miles, and, being a rich stake, brought forth the pick of the Western three-year-old fillies. In the books, Wary was the favorite, even money only being obtainable, Grisette meeting with much favor at odds of 2 to 1, presumably on account of Isaac Murphy having the mount. A great deal of money was wagered on the result, and when Wary's stable companion, Florimore, finished first, the agony was intense, as Stevens was expected to win with Wary."

The paper noted that Florimore won by 2 lengths, "although the general verdict was that Wary could easily have won."

Goodwin's Official Turf Guide reported odds of 5-4 on Wary, 8-1 on Florimore. "Florimore made the whole of the running and won by 4 lengths from his [*sic*] stable companion, Wary, who was pulled double," noted *Goodwin's*.

The *Live Stock Record* reported that Florimore won by 3 lengths.

Thomas H. also owned Treacy, an also-ran in the 1903 Kentucky Derby. But he "really didn't run his better horses in the Derby back in those days," said his grandson, Tommy H. Stevens, Sr., in a 1974 interview. "The Derby really didn't have the prestige it has now."

Another horse representing the Stevens family in the early part of this century was Wyeth, a promising colt who was sold to J. A. Drake and won the 1902 American Derby for him.

James Stevens, the father of Herb and Tommy, had a long career on the racetrack. "He was born in '73, and he started training when he was seventeen years old," Tommy recalled. "He trained until World War II. The help situation got so bad during the war he had to quit. So he trained for about fifty-five years, I reckon."

Of his father, Herb said: "He had a lot of good horses in his career. He had a horse called Siddons that was a four-mile horse back in those days. And he was a *good* horse. When Tommy first came out of the army, he bought a yearling and he named him Siddons."

The very first race that Tommy ever won as a trainer was

with Siddons—in the spring of 1946 at Keeneland.

Herb and Tommy, both natives of Lexington, Ky., learned from their father, starting out at an early age with horses.

"I've actually been racing and training since 1946, but before that I had broken yearlings and preliminary-trained horses back as far as 1934," said Herb, who was born December 2, 1916.

"I started breaking yearlings in the afternoon after school back in 1933, 1934," said Tommy, born February 8, 1919. "Soon after I got out of [Lexington] Henry Clay High School in 1936, I went with my dad."

In 1961, Marvin Gay wrote in *The Louisville Times:* "When World War II crashed onto the scene, Tommy Stevens asked to join the cavalry. He figured he knew something about horses. 'They put me in the infantry,' he said ruefully. Tommy was captured by the Germans during the campaign in North Africa and was a prisoner of war from Dec. 23, 1942, to April 29, 1945."

After the war, Tommy obtained his first trainer's license in 1945.

As fate would have it, the brothers went their entire careers without winning a $100,000 race until the summer of 1979. And when one brother won a hundred-grand purse, the other followed suit in less than a month's time. Herb won the very first $100,000 race in which he ever ran a horse, triumphing with Rockhill Native in the $125,610 Sapling on August 11, 1979. On September 2, Tommy won the $113,750 Delaware Handicap with Likely Exchange.

Herb, an all-around horseman, has liked to race close to home. He calls Keeneland Race Course "by far and away" his favorite track. A Keeneland fixture, Herb stabled in the same barn for thirty-five years until he was moved in 1981 to a barn that he has used since then.

Among his accomplishments, through 1994 he ranked as Keeneland's No. 6 all-time trainer with 137 victories and Churchill Downs' sixth-leading trainer with 238 career victories there. He won two races at the 1994 Downs spring

Tommy (left) and Herb Stevens. (Courtesy Keeneland Association)

meeting to take over the sixth spot, moving him ahead of Tommy, whose 237 victories now rank seventh.

Tommy, who died in 1985, achieved success in nine stakes at the Downs. At Keeneland, he triumphed 155 times to rank second on that track's all-time list.

In 1980, Herb trained Kentucky Derby favorite Rockhill Native. Many Kentuckians were rooting for Herb in the Derby. The veteran trainer, like his brother, was a hardboot in the truest sense, dedicated to the profession, proud of his heritage, and believing in hard work.

Rockhill Native was a gelding, and in 1979, the year that his star runner ranked as the country's champion two-year-old male, Herb expressed some strong opinions about castrating horses.

"I geld practically all of them that I race," said Herb, who owned 250-acre Haven Hill Farm in Versailles, Ky., at the time. "If I've got a yearling here on the farm that's going in a sale, naturally I don't geld him. But everything that's raised on my farm that I know that's going to go to the races, I geld them on the first day of April when they're yearlings."

And why did he do that?

"They're easier to get along with, they last longer, and if they ain't got enough pedigree to be a stud, why not make them just a nice gelding? That's the trouble today—if they'd cut about half of them, most of these damn, old cheap studs standing around, it would improve the breed. And not only that, we'd have more handicap horses if they'd cut half them suckers. Now every time a three-year-old wins any kind of stake, they talk about syndicating him right off—and that's the end of him."

Rockhill Native was the second racehorse ever owned by Harry A. Oaks. The first was Tony's Game, another stakes winner trained by Herb. Tony's Game won the $8,415 Apollo Stakes at River Downs in 1976. The loss of Tony's Game in a subsequent claiming race led to the $26,000 purchase of Rockhill Native at the 1978 September Yearling Sale at Keeneland.

"Tony's Game was a nice horse," Herb said. "He run pretty fast. He won a little old stake over there at River Downs and run five-eighths of a mile in :58, equaled the track record. But he finally got a little sulky. Anyhow, we raced him a couple of years, and then I let Tommy take him to Hialeah in the fall when he was a three-year-old and the first time they run him, they run him for thirty thousand and the man claimed him. So Mr. Oak asked me if I wanted to claim him back, and I said, 'No. Just let him have him. We'll just buy another one.'"

Recalling his purchase of Rockhill Native, Herb said: "Just like at any yearling sale, you look at a lot of yearlings and you turn them down, you look at a lot and don't get them because they bring too much. Finally, this little horse came along and I looked at him and I liked him and I told Mr. Oak, 'This is a kinda little old fat kind of a horse, but he's a sharp-lookin' little dude and looks like he might run some.'

So we followed him up there, and I bought him for him.

"And everybody's asked the question: 'Why did I geld him?' I told Mr. Oak, 'Well, we didn't geld Tony's Game, and we regretted it. I ain't gonna regret it with this one. We're gonna cut this dude.' Plus the fact that he was a kinda little old fat horse and I said, 'He'll just get fatter and be a little pudgy, bulldog-lookin' kind of horse. If we cut him, it'll fine him down some and that'll help him. And I don't know what his disposition might be, but it'll help that, too.' So that's the reason I gelded him."

Rockhill Native won both times that he raced at Keeneland—a 1$\frac{1}{16}$-mile allowance on April 15, 1980 and the Blue Grass Stakes nine days later. Winning the Blue Grass was an experience that Herb would always remember. "To me, it's been the greatest thrill I ever had because that's the biggest prestige race I ever won in my whole life, to start with," Herb said years later. "And the fact that it was there at home in front of the hometown crowd adds a whole lot to it. And the fact that I developed that horse away from the so-called big-shot centers of racing. So it all added up to a big event, as far as I'm concerned."

Rockhill Native entered the Derby with a perfect three-for-three record at Churchill Downs, having won there in his first three career starts in 1979—a 4-length score in a June 2 maiden race, a 3-length allowance victory on June 19, and a 2-length triumph in the Jefferson Cup on June 30. He went off as the 2.10-1 choice in the Derby and led for part of the race but wound up fifth under jockey Johnny Oldham.

Rockhill Native, a son of Our Native, ran nine times in his championship two-year-old season, winning six races and finishing second in two others. His final career record was ten victories in seventeen starts. Six of his triumphs came in stakes.

Herb has trained other talented horses, including Careful Manners. "He was a fast horse," Herb said. "Why, there ain't no telling how good a horse he was if he had been sound."

Careful Manners won fifteen of thirty-two starts in his four-year career (1970-73). He triumphed in the 1971 Flintstone Stakes and the 1973 Big Red Machine Handicap. The latter was a 1⅜-mile race on the grass at River Downs, and sixteen days later the versatile Careful Manners came back to win a 4½-furlong sprint on the grass at the Cincinnati track.

"He was a horse you could do anything with," Herb said. "Mud or dry, it didn't make any difference to him. Short or long. He was just a real natural racehorse. Good horse, if he'da been sound."

Careful Manners had so much ability that he just might have been the finest racehorse Stevens ever trained. "When you go on facts, you've got to say Rockhill Native was the best horse I ever trained because he's the only champion I ever trained," Stevens said. "But I've always said that if Careful Manners had been sound, he might have been the best horse I ever had my hands on. I entered him at Keeneland in the spring when he was a two-year-old. I blew him out for the race, and he chipped his knee. And we had to take a piece of bone out of him every year of his life up until he was six or seven—and he still came back and won races. He was a *good* racehorse. I'd loved to have had him sound just to see how much horse he was because he could do anything."

Herb said he believes he would have won the 1971 Kentucky Derby if a colt he trained by the name of Sea Levee had made it to the race. He was sidelined from the race with a broken leg.

"He beat some pretty good horses," Herb said. "I just thought that he was a real nice horse and that was a very ordinary year."

Sea Levee won the first three starts of his career in 1970 before finishing fifth as the favorite in the Kentucky Jockey Club Stakes at Churchill Downs. Sent to Florida and trained there by Kenny Noe, Sr., Sea Levee won his first two starts of 1971 at Hialeah Park. He went off as the 3-1 favorite in his first race at Hialeah and triumphed by a half-length. Finishing fifth was Calumet Farm's Eastern Fleet, who was to go on and run fourth in the Kentucky Derby. In his third start of

1971, Sea Levee came in fifth in the Bahamas. "He broke his leg," Herb recalled, "and we had screws put in and everything and then I got him back to the races that fall. We sent him back down there with Kenny the next winter, and the sucker broke his leg right off and had to be destroyed. But I'll always think I could have won the Derby with that horse. He was a pretty nice horse."

Tommy trained for such clients as George M. Humphrey, the former Secretary of the Treasury, and William H. May, who exerted much influence over the years on the Kentucky State Racing Commission.

For Humphrey, Tommy trained Likely Swap, a multiple stakes winner who foaled Likely Exchange. Tommy considered Likely Exchange the best horse he ever trained. Her record—twenty-three victories, fifteen seconds, thirteen thirds, and $475,140 in earnings—underscored her consistency and durability.

In her final career start, the 1981 Bewitch Stakes at Keeneland, Likely Exchange ran second to the outstanding Bold 'n Determined, beaten by just a neck. At the time, Likely Exchange was in foal, carrying Creme Fraiche, who would win the 1985 Belmont Stakes.

The '81 Bewitch was a thrilling race, one that Tee Stevens recalled in this fashion: "After Likely Exchange left the five-eighths pole, she started making her move, and they hooked up at the quarter pole. She ran up to Bold 'n Determined, and that's the way they came down the stretch. It was just nodding heads, up and down. They went head and head right down there.

"So they can say what they want to," Tee added with a grin, "but the Belmont winner was a graded stakes-placed horse before he was ever born."

Likely Exchange won seven races at Churchill Downs from 1976-80, including four stakes.

Stevens' first success in a $100,000 race—the 1979 Delaware Handicap with Likely Exchange—naturally was quite a thrill.

"It was very enjoyable," said Tommy. "You know how bad

you want to win one of those things, and when it finally happened, why, I was able to really enjoy it because she was just galloping through the stretch and opening up every time she hit the ground."

Of the other horses Tommy trained over the years, he called Cardinal Sin and Cactus Tom "nice horses—they just weren't top horses."

Tommy was represented in one Kentucky Derby, sending out Loyal Son in 1961. Loyal Son, who came in ninth in the Derby, went to the post ninety-one times and won twenty-four in a career that covered seven years (1960-66). A son of Hannibal, Loyal Son was trained by Tommy through his three-year-old season.

Loyal Son, a gelding, came into the Derby with a record of five victories, six seconds, and two thirds in nineteen starts. In his final Derby tune-up, the Blue Grass Stakes, he trailed by 22 lengths in the early going before finishing fourth, beaten 8¼ lengths by the winner.

"He was by a speed horse and out of a mare who had had a lot of speed horses and he looked like a horse who could run fast as hell," Tommy said. "But he wanted to come from last.

"We later found out that the secret to Loyal Son was he would run a series of good races for you, but when he started to tail off there was no sense in just letting up on him a little bit like you do most horses. You had to get him away from the racetrack and give him a little time off and just let him get out of the stall for a while. And he'd come right back and run good again. But it took a lot of trial and error to learn that."

Racing was just in Tommy's blood.

"I made up my mind when I was a young boy to be a horse trainer," he said. "It always appealed to me. I knew there were drawbacks to it such as having to leave home, but those were things that I knew I had to accept and so I never complained about it. As much as I love to be at home, when the time comes to go, I just get out and go and don't make a big thing out of it.

"I never learned any other business. For that reason, I don't condone anybody doing anything that's detrimental to the best interests of racing. I know there are plenty of people in this business who might want to fool around, but they've got another business they can go back to probably. But I don't, and I just don't put up with anybody who would do anything to harm this business."

Spoken like a true hardboot.

Nashua spent his entire stud career at Spendthrift Farm in Kentucky. (Courtesy Keeneland-Meadors)

7

Nashua: The Ageless Wonder

WHILE AN OLD HORSE STOOD off in the distance, an old man at Spendthrift Farm began a recitation that he had gone through countless times.

"This horse was the leadin' money winner of the world," the old man said in the spring of 1981. "This horse won $1,288,565. He won twenty-two out of thirty races. This horse is twenty-nine years old."

Meet Nashua, the Ageless Wonder. He was as much a fixture at Spendthrift Farm as Clem Brooks was himself. Brooks, the farm's head stallion groom, had been working at Spendthrift for forty years.

Nashua and Clem went back a long way. The two of them were pictured on a 1957 postcard that Clem proudly handed out to visitors, with his autograph on the back.

"Now we was a few years younger and a few pounds lighter, but that's me right here," said Clem with a laugh. "These postcards have gone all over the world. They've gone to China, they've gone to Japan, they've gone to Africa, Australia, England. Gone all over the world. Italy."

A visitor looking at the card asked Clem, "Who's aged more, you or Nashua?"

"I think I have, I think I have," said the seventy-four-year-old groom, laughing. "He's in better shape than I am. He's still makin' love. I done quit makin' love. That lovemakin' is hard on your *heart,* you know."

With that, Clem poked a visitor in his ribs and let out another laugh.

Nashua was a remarkable Thoroughbred, still going strong at the age of twenty-nine. "We figure the horse is something like ninety-six years of age if he were a human," said John Williams, then the Spendthrift Farm manager. "He's just incredible. He's as sound as any horse I've ever seen. He's a marvel."

Nashua was the sire of two 1981 Kentucky Derby candidates, Flying Nashua from the West Coast and Noble Nashua from the East.

The old horse had sired five previous Derby starters, but never a winner. Three of them had finished last—Narushua in 1965, Dominar in 1966, and Bombay Duck in 1975. The other two, Diplomat Way and Esops Foibles, ran ninth and fifth in 1967 and 1978, respectively.

Nashua ran in the Derby himself, finishing second to Swaps in 1955. Trained by the revered Sunny Jim Fitzsimmons, Nashua came back to beat Swaps in a match race, although the latter wasn't at his best due to a sore foot.

Nashua was voted Horse of the Year in 1955, and, after his racing days, he was retired to stud at Spendthrift. The main stud barn at Spendthrift was called the Nashua Motel. "I named it," said Clem, who considered Nashua his all-time favorite horse.

Not many horses live to be Nashua's age and those that do frequently are retired from breeding. In 1981, Nashua was being bred to thirty-four mares for the third straight year, slightly fewer than in earlier years.

"I would think it's a little unusual to do what Nashua's doin' now," said Clem. "But for *him,* nothin' is unusual for him. He's a fantastic horse. He's better than some of these youngsters we got around here."

Clem laughed. "You know what I mean?"

He walked down the driveway at Spendthrift, moving

closer to Nashua. "Right now he's all right to be around. But when he was young he beared watchin'. He would get you. He was a little treacherous when he was young."

Did Nashua ever get Clem?

"No, never did get me," Clem said, knocking on a wooden broom handle.

But Nashua once left a girl with a reminder. "She give him a kiss and he grabbed her right there [on her cheek], and I says, 'Don't you want to go to the office and see if they ain't got somethin' down there that they can put on there?' She said, 'Naw.' Said, 'I got somethin' to remember Nashua by.' I said, 'Yeah, you got a *great, big* blue spot right there.'"

And Clem roared again.

Nashua had some famous horses keeping him company at Spendthrift in 1981. In the paddock next to him was Affirmed. Right across the drive was Seattle Slew. Both were Triple Crown champions.

"He's always had this paddock," said Clem. "Once in a while he gets a little playful. When they turn them yearlings out over there, he'll maybe run a little bit. Not too much. He used to race a car up this way. Catch 'em down there and race 'em up this way."

Clem chuckled. "He always finished second." He laughed loudly. "Couldn't beat those cars."

Clem walked down to where Nashua was grazing in the paddock. The old horse was a bit swaybacked, but otherwise he was healthy and in fine shape.

"Come here, Mick, come over here," said Clem, referring to Nashua by the nickname he brought to Spendthrift from the racetrack. "Mickey, come over here. Hello, bud. Hello, son. Hello, buddy. How ya doin'? Huh? How ya doin'? Doin' all right? Huh?"

Clem rubbed Nashua on the nose several times. "This horse was a horse that you had to make run. He could run as fast as any horse on four legs—if you *made* him do it. Worked five-eighths of a mile in *fifty-six* seconds. Fifty-six seconds—that's, that's, that's burnin' oil."

Clem laughed again. "That's burnin' oil. *Fifty-six* seconds."

Clem recalled Nashua's Derby of twenty-six years earlier. "This horse lost the Derby to Swaps. The jock says he should have win the Derby on this horse but he rode accordin' to orders. Mr. Fitzsimmons gave him orders to watch a horse called Summer Tan in the race. Said, 'When Summer Tan makes his move, you make your move and you'll win the race.' But when he turned in the head of the stretch, he looked around, didn't see Summer Tan nowhere, say, 'I better take after this horse in front.' And he got beat."

Nashua Had "Great Ability"

Eddie Arcaro rode Nashua in the 1955 Derby and, in an interview in New York in the spring of 1981, he talked about that race.

"I think I zeroed in on Summer Tan," said Arcaro. "I had a right to. I didn't ride Nashua in the Wood Memorial. I was suspended at the time. Ted Atkinson rode him. And he just beat Summer Tan the last jump. I happened to be up in the press box watching the race. So who would you zero in on but Summer Tan?

"And I let [Bill] Shoemaker, on Swaps, have an easy lead with nobody bothering him and when I ran to him, I got to him at the quarter pole, but Swaps moved away from him. Beat him. Flat beat him. Naturally, if you could rerun it, naturally I'da run up and got Swaps. At least I'da went up the middle of the backstretch and made him go to running, because the farther you went with Nashua, the better he liked it. He could just run all day.

"Nashua could do anything. And I don't think I ever seen him take a deep breath—I mean, like being exhausted. He could run a mile and a half, he could run two miles. Never was completely all-out. He was an amazing horse."

But he wasn't Arcaro's favorite horse to ride.

"Fitzsimmons heard me knocking the horse one day, and he said, 'I don't understand why you knock this horse. The only fault he has is he keeps winning.'

"And he was right. But I was only knocking him because he would worry you to death. He'd have a horse beat and just stay there and keep the horse beat by a neck or a head but wouldn't run off and leave him. And I was always afraid something would come in behind whoever he was dueling with and beat both of us. But, of course, it never happened.

"He had great ability. He just never would put it all out, although he would win. He would worry the jockey to death, being me. He would beat a bad horse a neck or beat a great horse a neck or half a length.

"Nashua was probably the soundest horse that I ever rode," added Arcaro, who was aboard the horse in twenty-six races. "He was a horse that could work faster than most horses ever ran in their life. In the morning, he was such a free-running horse, and in the afternoon he wasn't. He wouldn't put *all* out. He would win. He had a lot of fight. When he would grab a horse, he would beat a horse a head or a neck, but he would never run away and leave him. He beat some awful bad horses just a little ways."

Of Nashua's twenty-two career victories, eight were by less than a length (two by a half-length, three by a neck, three by a head). On the other hand, he did win certain races by wide margins, including the Belmont by 9 lengths and both the Dwyer and his first Jockey Club Gold Cup (1955) by 5 lengths.

Bucked Cordero Off at Twenty-six

Angel Cordero, Jr., who rode Flying Nashua in the 1981 Derby, visited Spendthrift in 1978. He recognized some horses that he had formerly ridden, and, when he saw Nashua, he became teary-eyed. "I was very, very happy and glad that I could see him," Cordero said, "because I used to read about him when I was a kid—about him and his famous match race with Swaps and all that. And I never dreamed to see him *that* close."

Cordero did more than see Nashua.

Brownell Combs, the Spendthrift president at the time,

asked Cordero if he'd like to get on Nashua. "Mr. Combs said, 'Would you like to take a picture on him?' I said, 'I guess. I want to, but I don't know if he'll let me get on him.' He said, 'He'll let you get on him.'"

Cordero climbed aboard Nashua bareback. "The guy took a picture, and, as soon as the guy finished with the picture, he bucked me off. And I landed on my feet."

Zero for Seven with Derby Starters

In the 1981 Derby, the two sons of Nashua—Flying Nashua (a 48-1 shot) and Noble Nashua (71-1)—finished eighth and ninth, respectively. Later in the year, Noble Nashua won the Marlboro Cup Handicap by 3¾ lengths as a 12-1 shot, defeating Amber Pass (the second-place finisher), 1980 Belmont Stakes winner Temperence Hill (third), Pleasant Colony (fourth), and Fappiano (fifth).

Nashua finished 1981 ranked twenty-sixth in progeny earnings among North American sires. At twenty-nine, he was the oldest of any sire in the top sixty-five.

Nashua never sired another Derby starter, giving him a record of zero for seven with his offspring in the Run for the Roses.

Where Nashua failed to sire a Derby winner, Swaps was represented with one horse who wore the roses at Churchill Downs—Chateaugay in 1963.

While Nashua was siring seven Kentucky Derby starters, the rest of the '55 field combined sired only four runners in the big race. Besides Chateaugay, Swaps sired two other Derby starters—No Robbery (1963) and Ocean Roar (1969). Summer Tan, third in the 1955 Derby, sired Sunrise County (1962).

Nashua was known as a filly sire. He sired three winners of the Coaching Club American Oaks—Bramalea (1962), Marshua (1965), and Shuvee (1969).

Just as Nashua had won successive runnings of the two-mile Jockey Club Gold Cup in 1955 and 1956, Shuvee did the same in 1970 and 1971.

First Million-Dollar Racehorse

Author William Faulkner had gone to the Kentucky Derby in 1955, and in *Sports Illustrated* he used these words to describe Nashua after watching him on the track one morning: ". . . a drive and power, something a little rawboned, not graceless so much as too busy to bother with grace . . . appearing to skim along just above the top rail like the big diminishing hawk, inflexible and undeviable, voracious not for meat but for speed and distance."

Following his Derby defeat, Nashua set a track record in winning the 1$\frac{3}{16}$-mile Preakness in 1:54$\frac{3}{5}$. That summer, in a 1$\frac{1}{4}$-mile match race at Washington Park, he scored a 6$\frac{1}{2}$-length victory over Swaps, who wasn't at his best due to an infected forefoot.

On October 30, 1955, Nashua's owner, William Woodward, Jr., was shot and killed by his wife, who said she mistook him for a prowler. Late that year, on December 15, Nashua was purchased by a Leslie Combs II-led syndicate for a $1,251,200 sealed bid, a record price for a Thoroughbred.

On October 13, 1956, Nashua started for the last time, setting an American record of 3:20$\frac{2}{5}$ in winning the Jockey Club Gold Cup. Nashua, a big, robust horse, ran three times in his career in races longer than a mile and a quarter—and he won all three. He triumphed in the 1$\frac{1}{2}$-mile Belmont Stakes and twice in the two-mile Jockey Club Gold Cup.

In winning the Belmont, Nashua ran his last quarter of a mile in 24$\frac{3}{5}$ seconds. "His last quarter was really something," Arcaro said afterward. "That's the only time he really ran."

Final Public Appearance at Keeneland

Three days following his career finale, Nashua arrived in Lexington by train. Nearly one hundred people came out to watch groom Al Robertson lead Nashua from the railroad car to a van.

Two days later, on October 18, Nashua made his final public appearance—in an exhibition at Keeneland Race Course, near Lexington, Ky. It was proclaimed "Nashua Day" by Lexington mayor Shelby C. Kinkead.

Nashua, who weighed 1,090 pounds, was led around the walking ring at Keeneland. "Nashua was sound, unblemished, and high in flesh for a colt which less than a week earlier had run the fastest 2-mile race in the North American records," wrote Warren Schweder in *The Blood-Horse* magazine. "A few times he stopped walking and stood in grandeur, surveying the crowd, and his bearing in these moments moved Combs to remark, 'What a ham!'"

Wrote Len Tracy in *The Thoroughbred Record* magazine: "The gleaming horse, never looking better, was led some two dozen times around the ring as the crowd swelled around the enclosure and then banked ten or twenty deep on either side of the lane leading to the race course. After about fifteen minutes, Mr. Fitz called to Arcaro, who stood nearby in conversation with reporters: 'Eddie, come get your last orders!' Following a brief word from the trainer, Arcaro was boosted into the saddle, and the orange and blue silks of Spendthrift Farm were aboard the big horse for the last time."

"Nashua, 'Mr. Millions' to millions of racing fans, said farewell to loyal backers at Keeneland," turf editor Jerry McNerney wrote in *The Courier-Journal.* "Looking as big and magnificent as his imposing racing record, Nashua thrilled the fans with a brief flash of his vaunted speed."

"Arcaro walked the colt in the middle of the track the length of the grandstand, and loud applause followed them," Schweder wrote. "When they reached the end of the grandstand Arcaro turned Nashua around and walked him back to the club house, and again the applause followed."

Arcaro then turned Nashua and galloped the colt slowly through the stretch, around the turn, and down the backstretch. "Then at the quarter pole," McNerney wrote, "Nashua turned it on and the crowd thundered its acclaim as he raced to the finish line for the last time."

Nashua blazed the quarter-mile in twenty-three seconds.

"Even Keeneland, which has seen more than its share of

great horses, outdid itself," McNerney wrote. "It didn't roll out a red carpet but it did something more—it put in a public address system. It marked the first time in its 21 years that the track installed a 'P.A.'"

During the ceremony, Combs, Fitzsimmons, and Arcaro were presented with engraved gold cups. Nashua received a gold key to the city of Lexington.

"Everything points to another great career for him—that of producing little Nashuas to follow in his footsteps," McNerney wrote. "His sire, Nasrullah, standing at Claiborne Farm, is one of the most sensational sires of all time."

Tracy ended his story in *The Thoroughbred Record* by writing: "May his success at stud be equal to that he had in the fierce competition of the race track over the best his era could muster against him."

"Virtually Made Spendthrift Farm"

Nashua, who stood his entire career at Spendthrift, was scheduled to be bred to thirty-four mares in 1982, the same number as in 1981.

On New Year's Eve in 1981, the day before Nashua turned thirty, Spendthrift Farm threw him a birthday party. Brooks presided at the ceremony, leading Nashua a short distance along the shedrow for local television cameras.

The next month, with his health failing, Nashua was retired from stud duty and became a pensioner. Two weeks later, on February 3, 1982, he was humanely destroyed after his health had deteriorated and he was suffering from muscular problems.

On the decision to destroy Nashua, Arnold Kirkpatrick, the Spendthrift vice-president at the time, said: "We've been agonizing over it for about two weeks. We've been keeping him as comfortable as we could. But there comes a time when sustaining that life becomes contrary to the laws of nature and what's best for them."

Nashua was buried in front of the Nashua Motel, the main

Nashua in the snow at Spendthrift Farm in 1960. (Courtesy Keeneland-Meadors)

stud barn named in his honor. On July 18, 1984, a bronze statue of Nashua and Clem Brooks was unveiled in front of the horse's grave. The three-foot statue, which shows Nashua as a mature stallion being led by Brooks, was sculpted by Liza Todd, daughter of Elizabeth Taylor and the late Mike Todd.

Swaps died in 1972 after having stood the last five years of his life at Spendthrift. He was buried along a fence line near the Lions Circle at Spendthrift before his remains were reinterred in the Kentucky Derby Museum's Walk of Champions on April 16, 1986.

At the time of Nashua's death, he had sired seventy-four stakes winners, which ranked him sixth among stallions who had stood in North America during the twentieth century. Nashua's final figures were: seventy-seven stakes winners—or 12 percent—from his 636 foals.

"That horse virtually made Spendthrift Farm," Kirkpatrick said following Nashua's death. "He put the farm on the map. We've got horses who've been more successful as stallions, but I don't think any horse meant more to us."

8

Charting the Course of Derby History

JUST IMAGINE DOING your most important job of the year, one that requires you to communicate in detail with a fellow worker, and 130,000 people around you are yelling themselves silly.

That's the task that Cliff Guilliams faces every first Saturday in May at Churchill Downs.

Guilliams is the *Daily Racing Form* chart caller at Kentucky racetracks. It's his job to spot the horses at various points of the race, noting their position and how far in front they are (a head, half-length, length, etc.) of the horse immediately behind them. Afterward, he writes footnotes to accompany the chart, commenting on how each horse ran in the race.

This business of calling charts is an art, one that requires a dedicated professional, a stickler for details, a perfectionist. For the Derby, it's an especially challenging job that Guilliams and his colleagues face in their attempt to accurately describe the race, which usually draws such a big field that it resembles a cavalry charge. As Guilliams puts it, "You know how Custer felt if you've ever been in the situation of having a large field of seventeen or nineteen or twenty. If you've got a twenty-horse field, you've got twenty shots and you've

Cliff Guilliams at work. (Photo by Jim Bolus)

Jack Wilson. (Photo by Jim Bolus)

got to hit every one of them or you're going to get run over the top of. And that's the way it had to be with Custer."

Guilliams takes great pride in his work, especially so on the Derby. He knows that the Derby chart is being eagerly awaited by the press, so it's important to provide it in a timely fashion. But the chart isn't just for the readers of the next day's paper. It's for history, a record that will be relied on in the years and decades to come.

It's not an easy job, but Guilliams undertakes the task with preparation, pride, and a passion for the Derby.

With the Derby fields so large, Guilliams collaborates with another chart caller, Jack Wilson, the *Form's* supervisor of track and field operations, on the race's chart. Four eyes are better than two, and Wilson follows the first half of the field or so, with Guilliams calling from midpack to the rear. Afterward, they match their calls, similar to putting a jigsaw puzzle together.

Working hand in hand with the chart caller is a call taker. For the Derby, Wilson's call taker—in recent years his son, Jimmy—is on the balcony with him. Wilson also uses a tape recorder as a backup in case his call taker has trouble hearing him. A microphone, plugged into the tape recorder, is hooked to Wilson's binoculars. So far, Wilson has never had to go back and listen to the tape recorder, because the call taker has been able to hear him.

Meanwhile, Guilliams' call taker, Tim Holcomb, is inside the press box, and the two communicate through a headset that they use only for the Derby. For all other races, Holcomb is right alongside Guilliams taking down his call on a pad.

"The roar of the crowd is unbelievable for the Derby," Guilliams said. "There's probably 65,000 people on the grandstand side, counting the people that are walking around back in the garden areas, and then there are the thousands in the infield. What you're locked into is a wall of noise. And, unfortunately, some of the colleagues on our level still haven't read the book *No Cheering in the Press Box.*

"Tim is my right hand," Guilliams added. "He devised this

headset where we are on a single channel, locked in, where we can converse back and forth. He can sit inside the office and take it and not have to be bothered by the roar of the crowd. I can go in a conversational tone and not have to reach back and shout or scream. The louder you talk, the slower you talk."

Guilliams and Wilson frequently shorten the names of horses in calling them out. In the 1994 Derby, for example, they were saying "Go" or "Go for" instead of Go for Gin, "Strodes" instead of Strodes Creek, "Blumin" instead of Blumin Affair, and so on.

In writing down the calls, the call takers use the first letter of the horse's name. When there are two or more horses whose names start with the same letter, the call takers use a symbol or the first vowel in the name. "It allows you to go faster," Guilliams said. "It takes a special call taker to memorize that. We'll go out on the balcony together before the Derby, and I'll go through the field maybe five or ten times and say it out loud to him."

Wilson does the same with his call taker. "I want him to hear how I'm going to call the name," he said.

Leading up to the Derby, Guilliams prepares himself for the job much as a coach maps out a strategy before a game.

Guilliams, whom Wilson refers to as "coach," puts on his "game face" in the final countdown before the Derby. "I don't want anybody talking to me, I don't want anybody bothering me, I don't want anybody doing me any favors after the seventh race on Derby Day," he said, referring to the race preceding the Run for the Roses. "I want my space. I want to be mentally prepared to have the entire game plan where I've got it memorized and it's scripted—this is what we're going to do. There's no room for error, and we just go from there. It is exactly like coaching in a big game."

Guilliams tries to keep everything on an even keel, not showing any emotion at all, even though his insides are churning.

"If anybody tells you," he said, "that they can step out and call the Kentucky Derby, with all the emotion, with all the pressure, with the millions of dollars in stud fees in the future on the line, with the tremendous amount of dollars wagered—if they can tell you that they can walk out there and not be nervous, then (a) they've never done it or (b) they're a liar. Because it's impossible.

"When they play that song . . . you think to yourself, twenty years ago I was in high school trying to rig the blind draw for the Derby so I could get the winner. Or, where was I twenty-five years ago? Or, I remember this Derby, I remember that Derby. It's like a lifetime flashes before your eyes in the twelve minutes that these horses are on the track. It is a terribly, terribly, emotionally spine-tingling experience. You love it. It's better than Christmas Eve when you were five years old. But, boy, are you glad when it's over because there is an adrenaline rush that is immeasurable if you love this race."

Betting on the races might tend to have an effect on a person's judgment, but not so with Guilliams. "I don't bet on the races," he said. "That has never come into play with me having any problem with calling the races. The trouble I have with the Derby is it is *so* emotional."

For the Derby, Guilliams and Wilson make calls after a quarter-mile, a half-mile, three-quarters of a mile, one mile, the eighth pole (which is the stretch call, an eighth of a mile from the finish), and the finish. The Derby's first quarter is run in about twenty-three seconds, sometimes twenty-two and a fraction, and the last quarter in about twenty-five or twenty-six seconds (generally, the farther into the race, the slower the horses run), so you can figure out for yourself how quickly Guilliams and Wilson have to speak in order to call out each horse's position and the margin in front of the next horse.

The actual finish of the Derby comes from the photo-finish film, but just in case something would go wrong with the camera, the *Form* makes the finish call.

Immediately after the Derby, Guilliams calls the ABC television control truck and provides the order of finish, with margins, that the *Form* has called. ABC, in turn, produces the order-of-finish graphic for its national telecast.

Unlike their old-time predecessors, chart callers today

have the advantage of watching replays immediately afterward and thus can spot incidents that they might not have noticed during the actual running of the races. Although chart callers now have certain modern advantages that weren't available years ago, the profession itself hasn't changed all that much over the past century. This job still requires a knowledgeable person who is standing high up in the press box to train his binoculars on the field, call out the right horses and the precise margins—and do so quickly. It takes a keen observer, a good eye, and total concentration.

For a race of the Derby's importance, it makes good sense to use two chart callers. Wilson has called eleven straight Derbies, Guilliams six. Together, they provide the experience and expertise needed for the Derby chart.

"It gets a little uncomfortable after twelve horses," Guilliams said. "Fourteen is the next level, and then when you go from fourteen to seventeen, those additional three horses are just unbelievably different. If one man has to run through a seventeen- or an eighteen-horse field, you've got horses that change positions just like going through a revolving door. There are so many heads and half-lengths in there. In a race of this magnitude, you want the horse that is twelfth to be twelfth after six furlongs and the horse that is eighteenth to be eighteenth. It's just a matter of pride and conscientiousness that you want that to be as right with the fourteen through seventeen as you do with one through four when they come to the pole. And with TV and the still photos that *The Courier-Journal* uses, if you have any pride at all, you don't want your call and your chart to read any differently than what the public can see on a pan shot that ABC has or what *The Courier-Journal* has the next morning."

Guilliams, an Indiana State University graduate, covered the Derby for eight years for *The Evansville Courier.* But there's a difference between reporting on the Derby for a newspaper and calling the chart of the race. A newspaperman can follow one or two horses during the running of the race and not be concerned with the entire field. Chart callers, though, have to see the big picture, the entire race.

To see the entire race a chart caller obviously needs an unobstructed view of the track, and on Derby Day in 1993 Guilliams found himself in a rather difficult situation. It seems that the placing judges' stand is right next to the *Form's* office, and when the Churchill Downs Handicap, the sixth race on the card, was run, who stepped out of the stand and placed herself on the lower level of the balcony—right next to Guilliams, separated only by a railing—but actress Susan Lucci.

"She and John Goodman were in the placing judges' stand," Guilliams recalled. "She had on a white hat that was probably thirty inches across."

A big field of eleven ran in the Churchill Downs Handicap, and "when they came into the stretch, she started leaning over and this hat blocked the whole stretch view," Guilliams said. "To call the horses at the eighth pole, I had to back up a step."

Gentleman that he is, Guilliams didn't say a word to Lucci afterward. But he did say something to the placing judges. "I went off on that," he said. "I told the placing judges, 'This won't do.' They apologized. In the back of my mind, I had a flash that said, 'What if this had been the Derby?'"

The *Form,* which celebrated its 100th birthday in 1994, is known as "America's Turf Authority." Through the years, this publication has been referred to as the "Bible of Racing." It has faced competition at times, including the recent advent of Equibase (a company that compiles a national industry-owned data base of race results), but it is still acknowledged as the leader in its field.

Traditionally, members of the media have come to rely heavily on the *Form's* information. After the Derby is over, many writers are all but panting as they wait for the chart of the race to be produced and circulated throughout the press box. Without the chart and footnotes, some of the press would be in the dark as to how the race was run.

Guilliams knows how casual it was for him when he was covering the Derby for a newspaper, and he knows how serious he must be in calling the chart for the *Form.* "It's kind of like you're part of history, and the price you pay to be a part of it is not being able to enjoy Derby Day."

Sometimes, he even longs for the day when his job was more fun on Derby Day. "It is kind of a boy-I-wish-I-could-do-that kind of a situation—until it's all over with, until the chart is out, until the notes are out," he said. "And then you can sit back and say, 'Well, we did it again. We got it out. It was a good product.'"

That Secretariat Belmont

The veteran Wilson estimates that he's called at least 80,000 races in his career, including forty-five to fifty Triple Crown classics. Of all the races that he's called, Secretariat's 31-length victory in the 1973 Belmont Stakes sticks out in his mind. "Never saw anything like that before—*or* since," said Wilson, who in 1994 was in his thirty-ninth year of calling charts.

When Secretariat hit the finish line that far ahead, it was anybody's guess as to how far in front he was. Wilson, expert that he is, came as close as you could without hitting it right on the nose.

Mike Barry, a sports columnist for *The Louisville Times,* was standing next to Wilson in the Belmont Park press box during the running of that race. "What in the world did you call the margin?" Barry asked afterward.

"I made it 30 lengths," Wilson said. "What did you think?"

"Are you kidding?" Barry said. "I was so excited I didn't even know who was second."

Barry later wrote: "When the film strip came down from the photo finish crew, the strip that shows the exact margins all the way through the field, the official margin proved to be 31 lengths. I went back to Wilson. 'Jack,' I said, 'you blew it.'"

Wilson recalls that the only time he has ever editorialized in his footnotes was that '73 Belmont. He wrote that Secretariat, under a hand ride from Ron Turcotte, established a track record "in a tremendous performance."

Tremendous, indeed.

Bud on the Money

Even with a vested interest in the 1966 Kentucky Derby's fifteen-horse field, it was business as usual for Bud Lyon, the *Daily Racing Form* chart caller who had money on the victorious Kauai King. The Derby Day crowd sent Kauai King off as the 2.40-1 favorite, but Lyon had wagered on the colt earlier at much longer odds. "He had fifty dollars to win in the winter book at 50-1 on Kauai King, and he never missed a horse," recalls George Koper, claims clerk at Churchill Downs. "He called that Derby just like it was a four-horse field. He was a pro. Two or three of us knew he had that winter-book bet, and it never fazed him."

It seems that the next year, betting on the Derby winner *did* faze Lyon. Jerry Forke, longtime wire operator for *Daily Racing Form,* recalls that Lyon wagered on Proud Clarion in the winter book. As far as Forke can recollect, Lyon wagered ten dollars on Proud Clarion at 100-1 in the winter book at Caliente. Forke added that Lyon wagered additionally on the colt at Churchill Downs. "I know Bud bet a lot more money that day," Forke said. "I bet on the horse pretty good that day myself."

Proud Clarion, who went off at 30-1 in the Derby, was ninth in the early going before moving up to fifth at the quarter pole. Forke recalls that when the colt came charging down the stretch, the excited Lyon dropped his binoculars. He continued making his call "as well as he could without the binoculars and doing a little cheering also," Forke said. "I think we had to go over the replays for the stretch call."

Lyon triumphed in *The Courier-Journal* Derby Poll that year by picking Proud Clarion to win and naming two of the next three finishers. His second-place pick, Damascus, ran third, and he correctly selected Reason to Hail to finish fourth.

The Courier-Journal reported that Lyon worked for a newspaper "devoted entirely to horse racing" and that "he must have impressed his boss" with his Derby selection.

"If a raise is not forthcoming to Lyon," the paper said, "he probably doesn't need it anyway. He had Proud Clarion in the winter book at 50-1. He said he won $1,500."

Was It a Fair Call?

In the controversial 1957 Derby, Bill Shoemaker stood up at the sixteenth pole aboard Gallant Man, who was charging at the time. Shoemaker went back to riding, but Gallant Man lost the Derby by a nose to Iron Liege. Shoemaker later was suspended fifteen days by the stewards for "gross carelessness."

Lincoln Plaut, a Downs steward and former chart caller for *Daily Racing Form,* declared shortly after the Derby: "I think Gallant Man had to win by at least a length if Shoemaker doesn't make that mistake. You know he was going to win it in another jump anyhow."

Don Fair, the *Form's* chart caller for that Derby, likewise said that he was satisfied that Shoemaker's actions at the sixteenth pole cost Gallant Man the race. "It threw the horse off stride," Fair said, "and he was barely beat when he come up again."

Fair, a veteran chart caller, came in for considerable credit for noting the incident in his footnotes. It's highly unlikely that any other member of the Fourth Estate saw the incident, which happened so quickly that it would have taken a person with a trained eye and a lot of confidence in what he thought he saw to declare afterward that Shoemaker had misjudged the finish. It's even highly unlikely that Fair himself actually saw what happened. Keep in mind that it wasn't until 1963 that the Derby's patrol film movies were shown afterward in the press box, so in 1957 what you saw during the actual running of the race was all there was.

Certain insiders always contended that Plaut, after talking by telephone to Shoemaker afterward, thought of his longtime friend, Fair, and called him up to tell him about the incident. Fair, it was said, was in the midst of writing his footnotes, so the story goes, and once he heard from Plaut, he proceeded to pull his sheet of paper out of the typewriter and start over again, this time mentioning the fact that Shoemaker had misjudged the finish.

In recalling the '57 Derby, Fair was quoted as saying: "We didn't have films for that thing. I turned around and said to the man behind me, 'Did you see what Shoemaker did at the sixteenth pole?' I thought I saw Shoemaker stand up in the saddle too soon. We had to go down to a theater the next day to see the films."

If it's true that Fair "thought" he saw Shoemaker stand up too soon, then before releasing his footnotes he should have called the stewards for verification. Otherwise, he must have had a hard time sleeping that night while waiting to see the films the next day.

In 1973, I called Fair and asked him whether he had been tipped off by Plaut about the incident. Fair didn't admit to anything, saying: "There's no truth to that. I saw it myself."

But did he?

In 1982, Oscar Otis, a former colleague of Fair's, replied to a letter from me, and he had some enlightening comments about that '57 Derby.

"I was in the press box at the time and was on the *Racing Form* team—Fair, the caller; myself and Charlie Hatton, the columnists. It was one of the most tense press box dramas I have ever seen. The press crowded around Fair like a mob once they had the footnotes and demanded if it was right. Fair got up, tilted his head back, lit his cigar and said, 'The little boy missed it' and refused to retract. I said nothing but said to myself, 'Fair has got to be crazy to go out on a limb like this unless he knows something . . .'"

Otis commented on how difficult it would have been for Fair to notice the incident at the sixteenth pole.

"If you want to take a stopwatch and time a nine-horse field with a caller starting at the eighth pole, just see where he is calling at the end of 11 seconds, or even 12," Otis wrote. "However, there is a margin of a second or so—and, theoretically, it is possible that Fair could have seen it. However, his attitude in the press box after the race in sticking by his footnotes made me sure he hadn't; otherwise, he would have waited to see the pictures for himself before putting himself out so far on a limb—and a libelous limb at that."

According to those who knew him, Fair was a conscientious person, an expert chart caller, and a likeable man. He didn't seem to be the type of person to seek credit when it wasn't due him. So why would he have done so in this case?

Otis provided an explanation. It seems that Fair was put in a personal bind and forced to say he saw the incident. *Form* publisher J. Sam Perlman, who was at the Derby, had been pressuring Fair to give up his circuit—New Orleans in the winter, Kentucky spring and fall, and Detroit in the summer.

"Perlman wanted Fair in New York," Otis said. "Perlman was all over the place bragging about his crewman, and Don simply could not deny without making a jackass out of his boss. So why should he? Anyway, Perlman was so pleased with the outcome of the incident that, by money offered, he forced Fair to take on the New York tracks, and, by so doing, he could never admit publicly that he himself hadn't personally seen it. So nobody was talking.

"I knew there was a bolt missing somewhere, but even as close as we were, Fair never told me till the next year what actually had happened. He had been tipped by the stewards by phone, which is why he tore up his original notes and started again.

"This was later confirmed to me," Otis added, "by [steward Jack] Goode himself, who explained 'Somebody in the stewards' room made the suggestion we owed Don a favor, why not throw him a fish?' So the call was made. So Don was on firm ground when he made his footnotes."

A Fair Assessment

Native Dancer suffered the only loss of his twenty-two-race career in the 1953 Kentucky Derby. He finished second to Dark Star, beaten by just a head, after being bumped on the clubhouse turn. Don Fair editorialized in his footnotes, stating that Native Dancer "finished strongly, but could not overtake the winner, although probably best."

An Objective Observer?

Lincoln Plaut was the chart caller for the memorable "Fighting Finish" Derby of 1933, the race in which jockeys Don Meade, aboard the victorious Brokers Tip, and Herb Fisher, the jockey on second-place Head Play, reached over and tugged, pushed, and pulled as they desperately rode in rodeo fashion down the stretch.

Plaut started his footnotes with the observation that Brokers Tip was "much the best."

These were the days before the photo-finish camera, and one account stated that Brokers Tip won by two or three inches. Fisher always contended that Head Play actually won the race, but without a camera to prove him right, the decision was left in the hands of the placing judges, who ruled that Brokers Tip had won.

The margin was listed as a nose, so how could Plaut objectively have believed that Brokers Tip was *much the best*?

That's the catch. He may not have been the most objective person in the press box. In *The Courier-Journal* on Derby morning, Plaut's selections were listed as follows: Brokers Tip, Head Play, Ladysman.

Having picked Brokers Tip, Plaut took the liberty of stating that his choice was *much the best.*

I've interviewed enough people who saw that Derby to reach a different conclusion. Brokers Tip was anything *but* much the best.

Even Meade, the jockey who rode him, said that if Fisher had just ridden "his horse and left me alone, he's gonna win it hands down."

Altering History

In the 1924 Derby, the Downs placing judges were confused by the silks of Bracadale and Beau Butler. They placed Beau Butler third, but he actually finished far back in the pack. Jack L. Dempsey, the sharp-eyed chart caller for the *Form,* called Bracadale—not Beau Butler—finishing in the money. According to one story, Dempsey attempted to get the word to the placing judges before the race was made official, but his efforts were to no avail. The judges erred and named Beau Butler the third-place finisher. In order to conform to the official order of finish as seen through the eyes of the placing judges, the chart had to be changed and Beau Butler was listed as the third-place horse, slightly more than a half-length behind the victorious Black Gold. At the stretch call, Beau Butler was in tenth place, a full 13¼ lengths off the lead.

Dempsey's comments in the footnotes said: "Beau Butler closed a great gap and ran an excellent race." What else could Dempsey say? That Beau Butler was no factor but was erroneously placed third by the judges?

That Ol' Editorial Freedom

Chart callers in the old days editorialized more than they do today. If the old-timers didn't like something—the way a horse looked going to the post, the way a jockey rode—they said so.

In 1903, the footnotes for the Kentucky Derby's chart said that jockey Jimmy Winkfield "made his run too soon with Early, made up a lot of ground while rounding the far turn, but had nothing left when Judge Himes challenged." A week later at the Churchill Downs meeting, footnotes for a race declared that Rampooza, who finished fourth in a field of eleven, "needs a strong rider and Reed was of little help to him." The footnotes with the 1906 Kentucky Derby chart stated that third-place finisher James Reddick "was sore in his warm-up, but ran to his best form" and that Debar, who came in fifth, "was always outrun and pulled up a very tired horse."

The 1908 Derby was run on a heavy racing surface, and the chart's footnotes said that second-place finisher Sir Cleges "disliked the going and sprawled repeatedly, made a game effort to get into the lead, but the going was against him and, on a dry track, would probably have won off." The footnotes for the 1911 Derby faulted the ride of Roscoe Troxler aboard Governor Gray, saying that the runner-up "was allowed to drop too far back in the first half and, coming with a great rush in the last quarter, was going fastest at the end." In 1914, the footnotes for the Debutante Stakes at Churchill Downs said that Waterblossom, who finished second, "seemed slightly sore when going to the post, but ran a good race and made a game finish."

9

Sir Tristram Stands Tall Down Under

HORSE-RACING PEOPLE in New Zealand and Australia are very much aware that Sir Tristram has made an impact as the greatest sire in his corner of the world. But not all of those people are aware that this great stallion once ran in a race that is called "the greatest two minutes in sports."

I mean the Kentucky Derby, of course.

The Derby, which has been run continuously at Churchill Downs since 1875, is the most famous race in all of America. Sir Tristram didn't win his Derby, but he didn't disgrace himself either. He finished eleventh in the 1974 Derby, which attracted a record field of twenty-three starters for the 100th running of this classic.

Let's take a look at Sir Tristram's effort on that first Saturday in May of '74 and how well he's fared Down Under in retirement. . . .

Sir Tristram raced for his breeder, Raymond Guest, former U.S. ambassador to Ireland. The colt was classically bred, being by Sir Ivor, the 1968 United Kingdom's Horse of the Year, and out of Isolt, by Round Table, the 1958 Horse of the Year in the United States. Sir Ivor was by Sir Gaylord, a half-brother to Secretariat, the 1973 Triple Crown champion. Sir Gaylord was favored to win the 1962 Kentucky Derby, but he suffered an injury on the eve of the race and never ran again.

Sir Tristram entered the Derby having run in just four races, the fewest number of outings for any starter in that '74 Derby. As a two-year-old, he raced twice in France. He came out in his very first start going a distance of about a mile and one-eighth and won at Evry on October 11, 1973. Then, nineteen days later, at Maisons-Laffitte, he finished second in a race of about a mile. He won the first race by a half-length and lost the second by that same margin. He carried 123 pounds in the first race, 126 in the second.

Sir Tristram then was away from the races for almost five months, returning to competition on March 23, 1974 at Saint-Cloud in France. Carrying 128 pounds, he finished second, beaten a neck in a race of about a mile, but was disqualified to third.

The next stop for Sir Tristram was the United States.

On April 15, 1974, Guest, speaking by phone from his farm in Virginia, said that he had landed the riding services of Bill Hartack, whose five Derby victories tied him with Eddie Arcaro as the winningest jockey in the race's history.

Discussing his colt's initial victory the previous fall, Guest said, "Beat about twenty horses [twenty-one, to be exact]. Pretty good effort the first time out for a mile and an eighth, don't you think?"

Guest had no doubt that Sir Tristram could handle the Derby's 1¼-mile distance. "I think the horse will love a mile and a quarter, a mile and a half," Guest said. "I know he can handle the distance. I think he'd be ideally suited for it. He's a big, strong, sound colt."

Asked when he had decided to run Sir Tristram in the Derby, Guest replied, "I just was thinking about it all winter and thought to myself, what the hell, I might as well take a shot. It's the 100th anniversary, and so here we are."

Guest, running his horses in the name of his Powhatan stable, had been represented in one previous Derby. His highly regarded Tom Rolfe finished third in the 1965 renewal after receiving a criticized ride from Ron Turcotte, the jockey who later would pilot the legendary Secretariat. Tom Rolfe went on to be voted the best three-year-old of 1965.

Guest said he didn't intend to race Sir Tristram in the other two jewels in America's Triple Crown—the Preakness and Belmont Stakes. "If I win the Kentucky Derby, I'm going to ship him straight back and try for the English Derby, which will be a month later," said Guest, who had won that world-famous race at Epsom twice—with Larkspur in 1962 and Sir Ivor in 1968.

Guest sounded an optimistic note about Sir Tristram's chances in the Kentucky Derby. "I think he is a very nice horse. He's sound, and I think he's got everything.

"You hold your hat, now," Guest added. "I'm telling you, you're going to see a runner."

A week before the Derby, Sir Tristram ran in the seven-furlong Stepping Stone Purse at the Downs. With Hartack in the saddle and going off at 13-1 odds, he finished seventh in a field of thirteen, beaten 9¾ lengths by the victorious Cannonade. Four days later, Sir Tristram was timed in 36⅕ seconds in a three-furlong workout from the starting gate.

Sir Tristram was familiar with breaking from stalls when he arrived in America. "He started from stalls in all his races in France as a two-year-old and three-year-old," said his trainer, Charles Milbank, an Englishman residing in France. "He was maybe slow out compared to American horses but certainly not unschooled."

The Kentucky Derby was patterned after the English Derby, and fittingly enough, Princess Margaret and Lord Snowdon were on hand for the 100th running of the Churchill Downs classic. The race not only pulled in a record field, but it attracted a record crowd as well—163,628.

Judger and Cannonade, both trained by W. C. ("Woody") Stephens, went off as the favored entry at 3-2 odds.

Sir Tristram, listed at 30-1 in the *Daily Racing Form's* probable odds and 20-1 in the Downs program's morning line, was sent off at 25.80-1. The Downs program erroneously listed Sir Tristram as being bred in Great Britain; actually, he was bred in Ireland, having been foaled there on February 29, 1971.

Breaking from the No. 20 post position in the wild cavalry charge, "Sir Tristram showed a good turn of early speed," according to the footnotes in the *Form's* chart. He was third after both a quarter of a mile and a half-mile, dropped back to sixth after three-quarters, was eighth after a mile, eleventh at the stretch call, and eleventh at the finish, 11½ lengths behind the winner, Cannonade, who was considered the weaker half of the entry.

On the morning after the Derby, Hartack was quoted as saying: "I was pleased with the way he ran. It may be the first time in my life I ever was on a horse that finished unplaced and still was pleased with him."

Hartack said Sir Tristram showed that he needed more experience and seasoning. "On the turn, he just couldn't keep up," the forty-one-year-old rider said. "They ganged me and just ran by, but then in the stretch he was trying to come on again. The horses were just picking me up a couple at a time. He just could not keep at it all the way."

It's interesting that Hartack rode Sir Tristram in the Derby, because he's the same jockey who brought Northern Dancer home on top in the 1964 Run for the Roses. Northern Dancer, of course, went on to become the most successful commercial stallion of all time, and Sir Tristram has made a very big name for himself Down Under.

In an interview years later, Hartack was asked to recall Sir Tristram.

"I thought he was a nice horse," Hartack said. "Of course, that doesn't necessarily mean he's going to be a good stallion. But I thought the horse had a lot of potential, and I thought he was a pretty decent horse, but he never became acclimated over here because he was rushed to the Derby.

"When he came over here, he had never ever run on the dirt. I rode him in the Stepping Stone, and he ran bad—well, he broke bad, and, like I say, he'd never run on the dirt before and that dirt hitting him in the face, he didn't know what was going on. And then, of course, I did some work on him [schooling him at the gate] in between riding him in the Stepping Stone and in the Derby. I got on his back quite a bit after that, because I was concerned with him breaking.

"He was a horse who was a quick learner, because he broke well in the Derby and laid up close for about a half a mile or five-eighths of a mile, but he just wasn't acclimated to our kind of racing. I thought he ran a real good race in the Derby considering everything that was going against him. He just had never gone through the things that a normal racehorse would do in the United States in order to run in the Derby. So he had three strikes against him—never running on the dirt, from what I gathered he hadn't broke out of the gate [actually, he had] and then on top of it, shipping over. In those days, shipping over that quickly wasn't done very often. Of course, nowadays, they ship and they run and they run good. Then on top of it, he was a big, green, immature horse.

"He ended up beating half the field, so he never really stopped. Of course, I ran out of horse about the three-eighth pole, but he kept on going to where he ran a decent race. I thought he would have made a pretty decent horse if he had stayed here. He was a big, strong, good-looking horse, and I thought he had a lot of ability."

Sir Tristram's offspring have demonstrated a lot of ability as well. Since commencing his stud duties when he arrived in New Zealand in 1976, he has stood his entire career at the Cambridge Stud under the ownership of Patrick and Justine Hogan, who own majority interest in the syndicated stallion. He has been champion sire in both Australia and New Zealand in 1986-87; leading Australian sire in 1982-83, 1984-85, 1985-86, 1986-87, 1988-89, and 1989-90; top Australian sire of two-year-olds in 1986-87; and second on the Australian broodmare sire list in 1990-91 and 1992-93. (The racing season runs from August 1 through July 31 Down Under.)

Sir Tristram has been awarded the Dewar Trophy nine times in his career at stud. This trophy is awarded at the end of every season by the New Zealand Thoroughbred Breeders' Association to the leading New Zealand-based sire on combined Australian and New Zealand stakes earnings. This award has gone to Sir Tristram the following seasons: 1980-81, 1982-83, 1983-84, 1984-85, 1985-86, 1986-87, 1988-89, 1989-90, and 1993-94.

Sir Tristram has sired 108 individual stakes winners, including 40 who have triumphed in group I races.

His best runners, to date, are:

• Sovereign Red (six group I victories and joint second on the 1980-81 Australasian 3-Year-Old Classification).

• Empire Rose (the 1988 Melbourne Cup winner and leading filly on the 1988-89 Australasian 4-Year-old Classification).

• Marauding (winner of the STC Tooheys Golden Slipper Stakes and champion first-season sire in Australia in 1991-92).

• Grosvenor (three group I victories and sire of ten group I winners).

• Gurner's Lane (who completed a Caulfield Cup-Melbourne Cup double in 1982).

• Tristarc (champion older horse in Australia and winner of four group I races).

• Riverina Charm (four group I victories).

• Dr Grace (winner of four group I races and a $3 million earner in Australian dollars).

• Fair Sir (joint top on the 1986-87 Australasian 3-Year-Old Classification).

• Dalmacia (multiple group I winner).

• Tristangah (top filly on the 1989-90 Australasian 3-Year-Old Classification).

His sons who have proved successful at stud include Grosvenor, Sovereign Red, and Kaapstad. Grosvenor finished second to Sir Tristram for the 1993-94 Dewar Trophy.

On a visit to the beautiful green country of New Zealand in 1987, this writer learned that Sir Tristram has a temperament that makes his handlers *very* careful in working with him.

"He's a very relaxed horse, and he's a horse that's very adaptable," Patrick Hogan said, standing outside Sir Tristram's paddock. "He's a nice-natured horse, as far as a horse goes; once you've got him caught, you can do anything with him. But he can be a problem to catch. You can't just go into the paddock to put a lead on him and lead him out of the paddock.

"We have a system back here where we lead him into a big yard and catch him over the gate. Once we've got the bit in his mouth, we're okay and he's okay. Prior to that, he can be difficult to do anything with.

"As a three-year-old, when he returned from the Kentucky Derby, he smashed his near [left] fore pastern—he's got two steel pins in there—and he spent about three to four months in a box at Charles Milbank's stable in France. They had one little boy looking after him, and he used to sit in a corner and play music and talk to the horse. He was more or less there to keep the horse company, to keep him quiet while his pastern mended. Unfortunately one day Sir Tristram was getting more coltish and more playful, and he grabbed the boy by his shirt and then put his knees down on top of him and gave the boy a bit of a roustaround and injured him quite badly. From that day on, Sir Tristram's always known he can beat people if they allow him to beat them."

(In a 1993 letter, Milbank said he remembered no such incident with the stable boy and Sir Tristram. "I don't believe he ever attacked his stable lad and he certainly didn't injure him seriously if he did," Milbank wrote. "He was a bossy sort of horse but no trouble to deal with. I think everyone in the stable who rode him with some ability rode him at one time or another during his racing career. Perhaps he turned colty as he got older.")

For whatever reason, in 1987, it was clear to a visitor from Kentucky that Sir Tristram was not the type of horse you'd send to school for Show and Tell. "He's a horse that only two people handle—I myself and my stud manager," Hogan said. "He's never, ever served a mare, in all the seasons that he's served, without me there on the end of the lead. So if I'm not available, there's no service. That's sort of his temperament. He's very much a routine horse. We try not to alter the routine. If you do, he gets cranky."

Hogan's nickname for Sir Tristram is Paddy. "My father was born in Ireland, and, of course, this horse was bred in Ireland. My uncle's name was Paddy, so when I bought him, I said, 'Well, I'll nickname him after my uncle'—who was dead then—'and we'll call him Paddy.' And that stuck ever since."

Hogan went on discussing the amazing story of Sir Tristram's success Down Under.

Patrick and Justine Hogan admiring one of their horses in New Zealand.

"He's certainly been a fairy tale as far as our industry's concerned and for Cambridge Stud. He's done everything that he *possibly* could for us. He's been an exciting horse. I think he's lucky he stands at Cambridge Stud, because he's here forever. We'd never sell him. We've had offers. The day the horse walked off the plane from England, we did promise the horse he'd never, ever leave this stud farm."

Hogan added that according to his will, "If I die before he does, they're not allowed to move him from this paddock. He stays there. He'll be buried there. There's just *no way* that he'll ever be removed.

"The only reason that we really promised the horse he'd never leave Cambridge Stud was because when he arrived in New Zealand, we had a full book of mares; a number of breeders pulled out. They wouldn't breed to him when they saw him. Six shareholders pulled out and said they wanted their money back, which we did refund, because they said, 'Well, you've made a huge mistake here. This is a terrible-looking horse. We certainly couldn't stay in this horse. You've made a mistake.'

"So my wife and I just said, 'Okay.' We felt a bit sorry for him and a bit patriotic towards an Irishman. We just said, 'Right, you'll get our *best* mares for the next three years. We'll give you the *best* chance we can give you, and whether you succeed or fail, there's your paddock, there's where you stay.' So had he been a failure, he would have still stayed in that paddock until the day he was finished.

"He's amazing. To look at him conformation-wise, he's not built that he'd leave Golden Slipper winners. And yet he's left group I winners at all distances—the premier races. His fillies, his colts, his geldings, his chestnuts, his bays, his big ones, his little ones—there's no patent to them. They just seem to have all the heart in the world to win. There's been no actual patent of saying the individual you can pick is going to be a good horse, because he's left them all shapes and sizes."

As a racehorse, Sir Tristram didn't put together a sparkling

Sir Tristram at Cambridge Stud.

record. All he had to show for nineteen starts were two victories, six seconds, and three thirds. Exactly what was it about this horse that caused Hogan to buy him?

"It's fair to say that if you really took a quick look at his racing performances, you'd say he was way below average," Hogan said. "But I think if you took a very close look at each individual race and start that he had, the fact that he did win at a mile and an eighth as a two-year-old—it might not have been a great race, but it proved that he looked like he was going to have some ability over ground. One or two of his runs in France were very, very good, and I think, studying him individually for his performance, he did have a bit more potential in there, although one could say after a quick look, 'Well, he's done nothing.'

"And I think it's fair for people to do that, but I'd been to France and America and England and Ireland to look for a stallion, and I didn't actually get offered this horse and I didn't even see the horse. In fact, I was at Charles Milbank's stable and he was in the stall next door, but they didn't show him to me, they didn't think to offer him to me.

"It wasn't until I arrived home back in New Zealand and I was actually finished over there that a young guy from the South Island, New Zealand, sent me a pedigree and said he had a horse for sale on offer for around about 120,000 New Zealand dollars and would I be at all interested. And when I opened up the tabulated pedigree, I just couldn't believe what I saw. In that horse's first six generations, I could *not* find one bad horse, mare or stallion. He was double-bred to Princequillo. He was by a champion horse in Sir Ivor, which really appealed to me. He was out of the Hyperion female line. We all agree that Hyperion has worked in any country in the world. So really I bought him unseen. I bought him on a five-, six-generation pedigree. I was determined I wanted him.

"Certainly, a number of people said, 'Don't buy him.' But I just could not leave that pedigree alone. I was certainly determined to buy him, and I'm not saying that after the event. I could have very easily missed this horse because people tried to tell me I was making a huge mistake."

What Hogan made was a gigantic coup.

"He cost 160,000 insured and landed in New Zealand," Hogan said. "When I walked him off the plane and onto this property, the bill was 160,000 dollars New Zealand all up.

"His books have ranged anywhere from about 82 up to 108 for a season. Very, very good horse for fertility. He's very fertile."

In 1993, with Sir Tristram then at the age of twenty-two, Hogan said, "We're doing less coverings and are leaving it largely up to him. He's a very fertile horse still."

In the Southern Hemisphere's 1993 breeding season (August 1-December 31), Sir Tristram served 85 mares, and 75 tested in foal.

For the 1994 breeding season, Hogan said: "He's twenty-three, but he'll serve 60-65 mares. He's in extremely good

Patrick Hogan with Sir Tristram. (Copyright Thoroughbred Photos)

health and has shown, at this stage, no deterioration physically or healthwise at all. So he's a very young twenty-three years old."

One final thought from Hogan about Sir Tristram and the Derby (or the Darby, as they say in some parts of the world):

"It was good for me he didn't win the Darby. He'd be in Kentucky today if he'd won the Darby. So I was very fortunate he didn't."

10

Life Begins at Seventy-one

PERHAPS DIVINE INTERVENTION does have something to do with winning this thing called the Kentucky Derby. In 1986, the seventy-three-year-old Hall of Famer Charlie Whittingham won the Derby with Ferdinand, becoming the oldest trainer to triumph in this classic, which he captured again three years later with Sunday Silence. In 1990, the ninety-two-year-old Frances A. Genter won the Derby with Unbridled, the first horse she ever ran for the roses. In 1992, the eighty-two-year-old W. Cal Partee captured the Derby with Lil E. Tee, who provided jockey Pat Day with his first victory in the race after nine losses. And in 1993 the Derby finally came up roses for eighty-five-year-old Paul Mellon, who had many major races in America and Europe but had never succeeded on the first Saturday in May at Churchill Downs.

Mellon, the sportsman and philanthropist from Virginia, won the Derby with Sea Hero, who may have received a blessing in disguise when he started off the year as badly as he did in Florida. Then, on Derby Day, nobody in the Sea Hero camp was spotted back at the barn doing a rain dance, but a light rain before the race certainly didn't hurt the chances of this colt, who had demonstrated a fondness for a wet track. In a nineteen-horse field, a come-from-behind runner such

Mack Miller was beaming at the press conference following Sea Hero's victory in the 1993 Kentucky Derby. (© 1993 Churchill Downs Incorporated/Kinetic Corporation)

as Sea Hero might have encountered traffic problems, but not so. In fact, his jockey, Jerry Bailey, said that through the first mile or so of the race he had a "picture-perfect" trip. With a biblical reference, he said: "Every time I got to a bunch of horses, they parted like the Red Sea." Then when he did face an anxious situation at the top of the stretch, Bailey shot Sea Hero through an opening on the inside, and the Rokeby Stables colt did the rest.

If Divine Intervention had something to do with Sea Hero's victory, then it was only fitting that when his trainer, Hall of Famer Mack Miller, attended Versailles Presbyterian Church the day after the Derby, this native Kentuckian received a strong and prolonged ovation from the congregation at the beginning of the service.

Maybe the racing gods were looking after Sea Hero on Derby Day, but it was Mack Miller who was calling the shots on the road to the Derby. It was Mack Miller who had this colt on top of his game on the day that counted—Derby Day. And afterward it was Mack Miller who brought Sea Hero back to win the Travers in the summer, marking the first time in fifty-one years that a Derby winner had captured this prestigious race at Saratoga.

This writer followed Sea Hero after the colt arrived at Keeneland in the spring of the year. From a colt who was given little chance after two dismal 1993 races in Florida, Sea Hero was brought along perfectly by Miller. I have seen thirty-five runnings of the Derby, having covered many of them as a sportswriter, and I have never watched one colt as closely as I did Sea Hero in the weeks and days leading up to the Derby.

I work in the Keeneland publicity office during the race meetings, and when I first reported to the Lexington track in March 1993, I was told that Miller would have six stalls there that spring. On March 23, I called Miller in Aiken, S.C., curious about whether Sea Hero would be brought to Keeneland. I had lost track of the colt and didn't know his status.

Yes, Miller told me, Sea Hero would be brought to Keeneland. That was the only reason for coming to Keeneland, he added.

"He's doing fine," Miller told me. "There's going to be a big gap between his last race and the Blue Grass." He added that a decision would be made after the Blue Grass as to where Sea Hero went from there.

But let's backtrack for a moment and put this trip to Keeneland in proper perspective, and then when we take a look at Sea Hero's diary for the year, we'll see the different things that Mack Miller did to bring out the best in this colt.

Sea Hero's lone stakes victory before the Derby was the 1992 Champagne Stakes at Belmont Park. Later that fall, he was sent to Gulfstream Park for the Breeders' Cup Juvenile, but he didn't do well in Florida's hot climate. Or, as Miller put it, the colt "wilted like a flower" in Florida. "I think, too, he did not like the racetrack," Miller added. Sent off as the 2.40-1 second choice in thc Breeders' Cup Juvenile, Sea Hero dragged himself home in seventh place.

On December 6, Sea Hero was shipped from Aiken, S.C., to Florida to be trained at Hialeah Park by Flint S. ("Scotty") Schulhofer. Once again, the colt didn't adjust to the humidity and heat, according to Miller. The colt "just melted" in Florida, the trainer said.

"Scotty told me it took an awful long time for him to become acclimated to that climate," Miller recalled. "Finally, when we got to the races, he ran badly. Mr. Mellon and I flew down to see him run. He ran like a dog."

Sea Hero finished ninth in that February 7 race at Gulfstream Park, beaten 12½ lengths. "We were pretty discouraged," Miller said.

On February 25, Sea Hero ran third in a grass race at Gulfstream, beaten by a length and a half by Icy Warning, a filly. "So the Derby had kinda gone by the boards, as far as we were concerned," Miller said. "We thought it was over."

Schulhofer, recalling Sea Hero's experience in Florida, said: "Maybe he likes cold weather better. I don't think it was the weather that was bothering him as much as the racetrack [at Gulfstream]. He felt good, he looked good, he ate good. There were no signs of depression or anything."

Winning the Kentucky Derby isn't something a trainer can draw up on a blackboard early in the year, expecting everything to go perfectly every step of the way. Racing has its peaks and valleys, and from that low point of 1993, Sea Hero had only one way to go: up. In retrospect, running so poorly in Florida might have been a true blessing for Sea Hero. For one thing, it got him out of Florida and enabled him to go back to South Carolina, where he began to blossom.

"Luck is such an enormous factor in our lives," Miller said. "Not only to win the Derby but just in our everyday life—all the horses we train, there's a lot of luck to it."

With the stable's best-laid plans having been buried in the Florida heat, Sea Hero returned to Aiken on February 27. Shortly thereafter, he responded to the cool weather. It was a complete turnabout. "He just felt *so* good," Miller said. "He was back to looking like a racehorse."

A bit later, Miller said to Mellon: "Let's think about going to Keeneland and trying the Blue Grass."

"Oh, I think we should," Mellon responded.

Sea Hero was now back in the Derby picture, though he wasn't receiving any headlines or fanfare about it while working out at the Aiken Training Track. Knowing that he would have more than six full weeks between Sea Hero's last race and the Blue Grass, Miller "really got into this horse pretty good" on Aiken's deep track. "Among other things, he went a mile in 42 and 2 [1:42 $^{2}/_{5}$], which is an awful good move there," Miller said.

Miller, who keeps his horses in winter quarters in Aiken, races in New York for much of the year and maintains a home in Versailles as well. This veteran horseman had been down that road to the Derby before, but not in recent years. In 1968, he ran his only previous Derby starter, Jig Time, who finished sixth at odds of 36-1. In 1970, Miller entered Protanto in the Derby, but that colt was withdrawn due to an ankle problem. Both of those horses had prepped at Keeneland in the spring of the year, and Miller headed to the Lexington track for a last-ditch effort to prepare Sea Hero for the Derby.

Like many horses, Sea Hero thrived at Keeneland in the spring. "The weather was still cool, which appealed to this horse, certainly," Miller said. "And when you get out in the mornings after he's galloped and get out in the afternoons and pick some green grass, I think all those things are beneficial. Although they're only out for about fifteen minutes, there's something about being out of their stall and picking on something that they're supposed to be picking—grass."

On the morning of the Blue Grass, Miller said: "If he runs bad, we'll go to New York, and if he runs good, we'll go to Louisville. It's as simple as that."

Miller has established a reputation as a trainer of outstanding grass horses, having developed three national turf champions—Assagai (1966), Hawaii (1969), and Snow Knight (1975). In Sea Hero, he also had a horse who demonstrated ability on grass, twice winning on that surface as a two-year-old.

On fast tracks, which was the case in the Blue Grass, horses usually don't run with mud calks. These calks, pointed extensions or cleats on a horseshoe, are generally used for off tracks, preventing horses from slipping. Not certain whether he was trying to force a natural grass horse into being a dirt-track runner, Miller decided to run Sea Hero in mud calks in the Blue Grass. With his experience around horses, Miller sensed that Sea Hero, while striding out, didn't have as much confidence on dirt as he did on grass. "We do find that some long-striding horses get ahold of the track better with stickers [calks]," Miller said. "Mud calks do give them much better traction. I use them on a lot of horses. It does give them a much more secure feeling and more confidence."

Away from the races for a month and a half, Sea Hero obviously wasn't quite ready for the Blue Grass's mile and one-eighth. Considering that he wasn't in peak condition and didn't have clear sailing, he ran well enough, finishing fourth in that April 10 race. "He ran a helluva good race," Miller said. "He was beaten fair and square. He had a little trouble on the turn, a little trouble in the stretch, but he was only beaten 3 lengths. Had he not had to be checked a little bit, I think he would have been second. I don't think he would have won. But I thought that really his race warranted going further. And having the three weeks [between the Blue Grass and the Derby] was just what it took to get him up to where he should be."

Many Kentuckians were pulling for Miller in the Derby. Indeed, on Tuesday night of Derby Week, at the annual Kentucky Derby Trainers Dinner in Louisville, he received a standing ovation.

Sea Hero backed off his feed tub a bit for a day or two following a six-furlong workout eight days before the classic. "That goes back to his being a delicate horse physically," Miller said. "I don't think he has the strongest constitution in the world. You never know why that is. He's a big, strong horse, but he's out of a mare that's got some age on her. That might be a factor. I've heard that during my lifetime. But he's beautifully sound. Boy, that's half the battle."

Sea Hero bounced back, and by Wednesday morning of Derby Week confidence radiated from the barn. Coming off the track that morning, Sea Hero looked radiant. Horses can't talk, but anybody who was paying attention to Sea Hero on this particular morning could tell that he indeed was saying something: he was ready to run the race of his life.

At the barn that morning, Miller asked his assistant trainer, Danny Furr: "How did the exercise boy say he handled the track?"

Furr replied to Miller. I didn't hear the reply, but I did hear Miller when he walked past me and, leaning over, whispered in my ear, "Mmmmmm," almost as if he could *taste* the upcoming Derby victory.

In thirty years of making the stable rounds at Churchill Downs, I have never had a trainer do that. And this came from the conservative Mack Miller. At that point, I immediately quit trying to come up with a Derby exacta. My money was going right on Sea Hero's nose to win.

Recalling his feeling on Wednesday, Miller said, "[Sea Hero] had come back where he was eating well and doing well. And that's when I said privately, 'I may not win, but I've got some sort of chance.'"

Sea Hero could be a quirky horse when it came to handling certain tracks, and his stable was concerned with how he would fare on the Churchill Downs racing strip. "Churchill is a very difficult racetrack for some horses," Miller said. "It's not like the general run-of-the-mill racetracks. I guess the texture of the soil is different at Churchill."

Besides the track, there was the question of whether Sea Hero had the proper seasoning for the Derby. After all, he had raced but one time in more than two months.

While in Aiken, Miller had begun experimenting with different bridles and bits on Sea Hero, a colt with a habit of moving his tongue around in his mouth. "I think he's done it a lot of times," Miller said. "I think it's sometimes nerves." Moving his tongue in back of his throat could cause Sea Hero to gasp.

The trainer decided to run Sea Hero with a rubber bit holder, which theoretically keeps the bit up in a horse's mouth. The horse thus can't get his tongue over the bit.

Blinkers were taken off Sea Hero for the Derby in an effort to relax him. In explaining that important decision, Miller said: "At Keeneland, we abbreviated the blinker we had used in Florida. We had a very narrow cup with no hole behind. After the Blue Grass, we talked about it, and Jerry said, 'Let's take the blinkers off altogether.' So, he made the decision for me, and it was proper, and I have to give him full marks. Jerry felt he'd grown up enough to where he didn't need that equipment anymore. He was much more relaxed without the blinkers, and I think that was important in the Derby."

While in Kentucky, Sea Hero ran on Lasix, which commonly is used to control bleeding. Certain horses bleed from a ruptured vein—or veins—in the nostrils, the pharynx, or the lungs. Even though Sea Hero wasn't a bleeder, Miller used Lasix on the colt in the Blue Grass and Derby. "It's a diuretic, and it lowers the blood pressure," Miller explained. "I take a diuretic every day of my life for blood pressure. You take a horse that's really nervous and walks in the paddock washy, Lasix will help him immensely."

As a three-year-old, Sea Hero wasn't a supernervous horse who walked into the paddock the way a man goes to the electric chair, all quivering and shaking, but Miller did describe the colt as being "a little hyper."

The trainer noted: "He's out of a Graustark mare. Graustark was by Ribot, and that's about as hot a blood as you can get."

On Derby Day, a light rain for approximately thirty minutes stopped about a half-hour before post time for the big race. The racing strip—fast, but wet—should have brought smiles to the faces of those who bet on Sea Hero, whose victory in the Champagne the previous fall had come on an off track.

Sea Hero, who ran with mud calks in the Derby, was listed at 30-1 in the program's morning line but went off at 12-1. If all the bettors had seen him on his walk over from the stable area to the paddock, he no doubt would have gone off at a shorter price. Looking like a million dollars, he was truly the "now" horse for the Derby.

Sea Hero was ready, and the track was wet. All he needed was clear sailing.

Breaking from the No. 6 post position, the colt was back in thirteenth place as the bulky field raced past the twin-steepled grandstand the first time. Those watching him noticed that his action wasn't right. He was "climbing"—holding his head higher than normal and high-stepping with his forelegs, as if he were climbing a ladder. "Down through the stretch the first time, boy, his head was in the air and he was climbing *awful,*" Miller said. "I told Mr. Mellon, 'This horse is really uncomfortable.' I was hoping he would adapt to it. He did. It's a long way, you know. Down the backside, you could see him level off and you could tell that he was going to run more than he had in the past. He was trying to run. He was an honest horse that day."

Afterward, at a press conference, the seventy-one-year-old Miller, who has trained for Mellon since 1977, said: "I really never thought I'd win the Derby. I thought my time was running out. But I have this marvelous owner, who is patient and kind and breeds very, very nice horses. I'm thrilled to death for him. I'm not important, but he is."

An interviewer told Miller: "So being a Kentuckian, a lot of feeling goes into this race."

To which Miller replied: "It's the greatest—this is the best. It makes you want to cry a bit."

Two weeks later, Sea Hero ran a disappointing fifth in the Preakness. "I think having two races in the space of fourteen days was really not his cup of tea," Miller said.

Neither was the track condition at Pimlico. "When you have to wait forty or fifty minutes between races and you have this nice, gentle breeze blowing about fifteen or twenty miles an hour on a beautiful day when there was *no* humidity at all, the track tends to dry out," Miller said.

Everything came up right for Sea Hero in his next start, the Belmont. He was racing on his home track, and the track was off. But the inconsistent colt bombed, finishing seventh.

"I thought the horse came up to the race as good as possible," Miller said two days later. "We got the rain we wanted right at the proper time. But it just didn't work. The plan was to tuck back and cover him up so he could run where he's supposed to run. But he was terribly rank. I think he just expended all his energy early on.

"Another interesting thing," Miller added, "is that Jerry said when he pulled up, he was gurgling—like he had gotten his tongue over the bit. I don't know whether that's valid or not, but in the future we'll probably run him in a tongue tie [a bandage or rubber band used to tie a horse's tongue down]."

When Sea Hero returned to action in the Jim Dandy on August 1, Miller indeed had abandoned the rubber bit holder and gone to a tongue tie. Miller said that at the time of the Derby he thought the bit holder had helped. "But by the same token, when he was pulling up, he still made somewhat of a gurgling noise. He kept playing with his tongue, and I think it kept him from breathing properly. He was gagging a bit, so to speak."

Beginning with the Jim Dandy, Miller also used a shadow roll (a heavy sheepskin covering placed over the nose band designed to minimize the effect of ground shadows) on Sea Hero. "Most of my horses run in shadow roll," Miller said. "I use it because I think it breaks some of the sand hitting them in the face."

In the Jim Dandy, Sea Hero ran fourth, beaten 7½ lengths by the winner, Miner's Mark, who carried 9 fewer pounds than the Rokeby colt (126-117). It wasn't a bad race for Sea Hero, considering the weights and the fact that he had been off for two months.

Earlier in the spring, Sea Hero had gone from fourth in the Blue Grass to first in the Derby, and in the summer he did the same thing, improving from fourth in the Jim Dandy to first in the Travers, which was run on a fast track. In both cases, leading up to his fourth-place finishes in the Blue Grass and the Jim Dandy, Sea Hero had been off from competition for a while.

Winning the Travers was an impressive feat because usually a horse can't have it both ways. He can't be good enough in the spring to win the Derby and come back in the summer to get the job done in the Travers. The last Derby winner to pull off that double was Shut Out in 1942. Running in all three Triple Crown races is extremely demanding, taking so much out of horses that sometimes they're never quite the same again. But Miller, who knows his stuff, was able to bring Sea Hero back in splendid fashion for the Travers.

Miller ran Sea Hero with turndown shoes (rear calks) in the Travers, the first time the trainer had used that type of shoe on a racehorse. With these shoes, the stickers are turned down (some at moderate degrees, others more sharply) and work as a cleat to provide extra traction.

Some observers thought the turndowns played a role in Sea Hero's victory, but Miller believed instead that a training technique was more important. Leading up to the Travers, Miller employed a form of interval training "a time or two" with Sea Hero. In this training method, horses work out, then are rested before working out again. In Sea Hero's case, Miller worked the colt short distances—just a quarter of a mile.

"I have had horses who want to hold their breath," Miller explained. "Jerry never told me he held his breath, and I don't think he did. But when he was pulling up after his races, he was gagging a bit, making a noise, and between the Jim Dandy and the Travers I did some interval training with him. It's not interval training in the truest sense. What we did was we put a very sharp quarter-of-a-mile work into him on his work day and then brought him back to the paddock at Saratoga and walked him for twenty-five minutes and just let him sort of relax and cool out there, with the weight up. We took him back, galloped around, and broke him the second time—a very sharp quarter. He went sharper the second time than he did the first. In the Travers, when he got to the half-mile pole, instead of giving it up, so to speak, he took hold of the bit and took off. And I am sure, in my own mind, that the interval training had a lot to do with his win."

Sea Hero ran one more time as a three-year-old, finishing third in the Molson Export Million on September 19 in Canada. He wore turndown shoes in that race, proof that they couldn't work magic.

A calcium deposit subsequently put Sea Hero on the sidelines for the rest of the year.

"It was just a little calcium deposit—it looked like a little sand pile—above the joint on the left knee," Miller explained. "It's not in the articulating surface, it's not in the joint—which is very, very important. No chips, no fractures. He

Sea Hero charged to victory in the 1993 Travers. He became the first horse since Shut Out in 1942 to win both the Kentucky Derby and Travers. (Courtesy New York Racing Association)

didn't take a bad step in Canada. But we felt that we should not go further."

Many other trainers might have pushed on with a horse suffering from the same problem, but not the ever-cautious Miller. "If you're honest with yourself, you know that he can't do as well as he should do," Miller said. "And the mere fact that he had had a hard campaign, it was time to stop."

Miller, who brought Sea Hero back to the races in 1994, has one advantage over other trainers. He trains for Paul Mellon.

"I work for an unusual person," Miller said. "That's well documented. It's written in stone that he gives you all the necessary time. He doesn't get on the telephone and say, 'Boy, you're awful slow.' I have the privilege of taking my time and doing what's best for the horse. I'm not always right, but I have a better chance of being right working for a man who understands. He's an awfully well informed owner. When the horses go wrong, they need rest. We give them the necessary rest."

Rushing the colt to get to the Derby "took its toll," Miller thought in hindsight. "He didn't have the bottom under him that the other horses had had. So maybe all these things told in the end, who knows.

"There's *enormous* pressure when you have to start in mid-January to get a horse ready to run the first day of May—get him seasoned enough and have him sound enough where you haven't hurt him. Horses get hurt when they get tired. When you have to go through all this preparatory racing to get there on May 1st, it's an enormous chore."

Miller has trained champions and, before May 1, 1993, he had won many major races. But he'll always be remembered first and foremost for winning the 119th Derby with Sea Hero. It's a distinction he'll carry with him the rest of his life.

"I think it's every trainer's dream to win the Derby, *especially* if you're a Kentuckian," he said. "I've had such a great life. And to cap it this way, it's a fairy tale."

Did Miller say something about capping his life in 1993?

Two days after the Travers, this bona fide Kentuckian came to Louisville to be inducted into the Kentucky Athletic Hall of Fame. "There is a perception in this country that life begins at forty," Miller said in his opening remarks. "Wrong, absolutely wrong. It begins at seventy-one."

Spend a Buck, ridden by Angel Cordero, Jr., charged to a 5¼-length victory in the 1985 Kentucky Derby. (© Churchill Downs Incorporated/Kinetic Corporation)

11

Spend a Buck: A Horse Who "Lived to Race"

ENTERING THE PADDOCK for the 1985 Monmouth Handicap with horseman William S. Farish, Dennis Diaz couldn't help but notice the main competition that their colt, Spend a Buck, would face that afternoon.

"Carr de Naskra was led right by us," Diaz recalled. "We were thirty or forty feet away from him. I looked at him and then looked over at Will, who had purchased half of Spend a Buck to syndicate him at that point, and I said, 'Will, we've got a problem today. That horse looks like he just stepped off a Richard Stone Reeves painting.' That was the most beautifully conditioned horse that I had probably seen that entire season. He was gorgeous. He was dappled out. You could tell by his attitude and by the way he carried himself that he was ready to race that day."

Carr de Naskra certainly did have his running shoes on that afternoon, but so did Spend a Buck. After a furious battle to the wire with Carr de Naskra, Spend a Buck won by a nose in track-record time of 1:46⅘ for the mile and one-eighth. Spend a Buck, favored at 1-2, carried 118 pounds and conceded weight on the scale to his older opponents, including the four-year-old Carr de Naskra (120).

As memorable as the Monmouth Handicap was, Diaz believes Spend a Buck actually ran his greatest race earlier in the season in the Jersey Derby.

In 1985, Garden State Park offered a $2-million bonus for a horse sweeping the Cherry Hill Mile, Garden State Stakes, Kentucky Derby, and Jersey Derby. Spend a Buck had captured the first three races in the series, and, in a controversial decision, his stable elected to run the colt in the Jersey Derby instead of the Preakness, the traditional next start for a winner of the Run for the Roses.

"One of the reasons that we skipped the Preakness was the extra nine days," Diaz said. "We had run that horse four times in six weeks. Those extra nine days really meant a lot to us."

Spend a Buck won the bonus, but he had to do it the old-fashioned way. He had to earn it every step of the way in the 1¼-mile Jersey Derby. Facing repeated challenges, he had the determination and class to win. He stumbled at the start, and Huddle Up ran with him for almost seven furlongs. Spend a Buck then took shots from Creme Fraiche and El Basco. Creme Fraiche, who would win the Belmont Stakes in his next start, moved through on the inside and actually held the lead briefly near the quarter pole, but Spend a Buck came back to beat him by a neck as the 1-20 favorite.

"Today, he showed how much horse he really is," his trainer, Cam Gambolati, said afterward. "They tried him today like he's never been tried before, and he was still game enough to win it. You can count on one hand the number of horses who ran six furlongs in 1:09 and went on to win a mile and a quarter after they had been challenged early and late."

"It was a tough race," Diaz said, "and he didn't have the easiest of trips. There's no question he showed the heart of a champion. He came through the race with nicks and cuts and bruises. He got bumped around pretty good."

Years later, Diaz would look back on the '85 Jersey Derby and say, "I thought it was his greatest race. He had a difficult start, and Huddle Up forced him to run. They ran the first three-quarters of a mile in 1:09 flat. Everybody thought that he was absolutely cooked at that point."

And then along came Creme Fraiche. "Woody Stephens had Creme Fraiche at the top of his game," Diaz said.

Diaz pointed out that Spend a Buck was headed "not once, but twice" by Creme Fraiche. "Watch the video," he said.

Coming back to win the Jersey Derby "showed his guts," Diaz said. "He just had a lot of heart."

He had a lot of intelligence, too. Diaz spotted that intelligence in 1983 while inspecting a group of horses for sale in Kentucky. He noticed a Buckaroo colt who sought the assistance of a "bodyguard," a big, rawboned colt sired by Junction. There were about thirty or so yearlings in a paddock, all running loose without halters, and Diaz recalled, "Every time a horse made a run at this one colt or would get after him, he'd put that Junction colt between himself and the other horses. And every time we'd get up to try to take a good, close look at him, he'd run around behind that Junction colt."

Diaz saw the actions of the Buckaroo colt as a sign of intelligence. "He knew how to take care of himself," said Diaz, who liked what he saw of the yearling and paid $12,500 for him.

Named Spend a Buck, the colt developed into the 1985 Horse of the Year.

As a two-year-old, Spend a Buck won the Arlington-Washington Futurity and Miller High Life Cradle Stakes. After suffering a chip in his right knee, he underwent arthroscopic surgery on November 26, 1984, a twelve-minute operation sixteen days following a third-place finish in the inaugural Breeders' Cup Juvenile at Hollywood Park.

Spend a Buck finished third in his 1985 debut, the Bay Shore at Aqueduct, and then won the Cherry Hill Mile by 10½ lengths. He entered the Kentucky Derby off a blazing victory in the 1⅛-mile Garden State Stakes. His time of 1:45⅘ was just two-fifths of a second off the world record.

Gambolati termed Spend a Buck's victory in the Garden State Stakes as "awesome." The colt led by 6 lengths at the stretch call and was ridden out to win by 9½. "The first part of it, he did it on his own," said his jockey, Angel Cordero, Jr. "When he got to the quarter pole, I asked him to run. He finished good. He was as strong at the finish as he was at the start. It was one fantastic race for him."

In the Kentucky Derby, Spend a Buck had the lead all to himself after Eternal Prince, who was expected to hook up with him in an early speed duel, got off to a bad start. Running on a hard track, Spend a Buck led through six furlongs in $1{:}09\frac{3}{5}$ and a mile in $1{:}34\frac{4}{5}$, the fastest fractions for those distances in Derby history. Normally, a horse would wilt under such a demanding pace, but not Spend a Buck. He was far ahead and running unchallenged on the lead, and there was no catching him down the stretch. Ridden by Cordero, he hit the wire $5\frac{1}{4}$ lengths in front in a remarkable performance. His $2{:}00\frac{1}{5}$ for the mile and a quarter was the third-fastest time ever for a Derby winner. Two of his Derby victims would win the Breeders' Cup Classic—Proud Truth in 1985 and Skywalker in 1986.

In his next race, the Jersey Derby, Spend a Buck picked up the bonus and a $600,000 first-place check, making it a $2.6-million payday, the most ever awarded after a single race.

Following a two-month layoff, Spend a Buck made his next appearance in the Haskell Invitational Handicap at Monmouth Park. Eleven days before the Haskell, he turned in a sparkling workout between races at Monmouth. The work was reported as a mile in $1{:}34\frac{3}{5}$, matching the track record, but Gambolati said that the colt actually worked seven furlongs in 1:22 and galloped out the mile in $1{:}34\frac{3}{5}$. That workout, Gambolati said, "was the most impressive thing I've ever seen a horse do."

Spend a Buck finished second in the Haskell, losing by $3\frac{3}{4}$ lengths to Skip Trial, a 35-1 long shot. Spend a Buck carried 127 pounds, 11 more than the winner.

In his next race, Spend a Buck won the Monmouth Handicap and then was scheduled to start in the Pennsylvania Derby, but after a workout a filling was discovered in his right front ankle and he was retired.

Spend a Buck, a beautifully proportioned horse, was retired to Lane's End Farm with earnings of $4,220,669, second on the all-time list to John Henry's $6,597,947. Spend a Buck was never out of the money in fifteen career starts. Cordero rode him in his last two starts of 1984 and his first four of 1985. Laffit Pincay, Jr., was Spend a Buck's jockey in his last three races.

"He has done everything as a racehorse that he needs to do," Diaz said at the time of the colt's retirement. "We feel this decision is in his best interests. We had hoped to run him next season as a four-year-old, but he injured his right ankle in a blowout for the Pennsylvania Derby. There has been a lot of wear and tear along the way, and we just felt this was the right thing to do."

Following the announcement that Spend a Buck had been voted 1985 Horse of the Year, Diaz said: "He lived to race. He loved to go out there on Saturday afternoon and race. He had as much courage as any horse who ever stepped on a track. And he was very intelligent. We didn't have to make him do anything. He always did what was right."

The famous Fighting Finish photograph taken by Wallace Lowry shows jockey Don Meade on Brokers Tip (right) and Herb Fisher on Head Play as they neared the finish. (Courtesy *The Courier-Journal*)

12

That Fighting Finish Photo

Wallace Lowry had no idea when he headed out to Churchill Downs on May 6, 1933, that he was going to take a picture that would forever be a part of Kentucky Derby lore.

Lowry had to be just hoping that his picture would turn out—nothing more. After all, he had been assigned to take the same type of photograph for *The Courier-Journal* the year before, and he blew it. His assignment was to snap a head-on photograph of the Derby's stretch run, taking the picture while lying on the ground and shooting up at the horses.

But Lowry didn't blow it in 1933. Not only did he photograph the horses coming down the stretch, but he happened to be taking a picture of one of the most dramatic moments in Derby history. He couldn't have foretold that afternoon that two jockeys would ride down the stretch as if they were drunk, or that his picture would spin off many legends, including the belief (would you believe?) that Lowry *himself* was drunk on the job.

Rumors that are perpetuated through the years have a way of being accepted as fact, but it's a safe bet that Lowry wasn't drunk. He was drinking maybe but certainly was sober enough to handle his job professionally.

The 1933 renewal was just another Derby for slightly more

than a mile, and then the most controversial homestretch battle in the history of the race began to unfold. When it did, Lowry was ready to photograph an intense duel between two roughriding jockeys who were clearly interfering with each other by pushing and pulling as they desperately drove their horses toward the finish line.

The race came to be known as the Fighting Finish and, if there was ever a picture that was worth a thousand words, it was Lowry's.

Other pictures were taken of that finish—still photos and films—but those were all from the side. It took a head-on shot to tell the story, and that's what Lowry snapped.

The photograph was shot with the camera on the ground and with the daring Lowry actually on the racetrack, only a short distance from the pounding hoofs of Brokers Tip, the inside horse ridden by Don Meade, and Head Play, with Herb Fisher up.

The stark black-and-white photograph shows Fisher reaching far over with his left hand, grasping the saddlecloth of Brokers Tip. Meade, meanwhile, is reaching out with his right hand at Fisher's shoulder. Closer inspection also reveals the left rein of Head Play hanging slack. An added touch to the photo is the presence of one of the twin spires off to the left.

Lowry died twenty-four years after the 1933 Derby, but Meade and Fisher attended the Run for the Roses in 1983, the fiftieth anniversary of the Fighting Finish. Meade, sixty-nine, and Fisher, seventy-two, were friends then. As fate would have it, they lived just a mile or so from each other in Hollywood, Fla., and they traveled together to and from the Derby. The old boys behaved themselves that time in Louisville.

It's too bad Wally Lowry wasn't around to be part of the celebration. For it was his picture, more than anything else, that called attention to the battle between the two jockeys and forever identified them as the two riders involved in this unforgettable Derby.

"If it wasn't for his photo, no one would have ever known

actually what happened," Meade said. "Why, hell, if he didn't get it, no one could have said a damn thing. Nobody would have known what the hell they were talking about. It would be a guess-and-guess thing."

Lowry's photograph is the single most famous picture in Derby history. Some believe it's the best racing, or even *sports,* picture ever taken.

The 1933 Derby's wild stretch battle started after Charlie Corbett, who was riding a horse named Charley O., hollered to Fisher in the upper stretch: "Watch out for the inside!"

Fisher glanced to his inside and, lo and behold, here came Brokers Tip slipping up into contention.

In an instantaneous decision that would leave him stamped the rest of his life as one of the Fighting Finish jockeys, Fisher guided Head Play, who was leading, over to the inside, closer and closer to the charging Brokers Tip. Before introductions could be made between the two horses, Meade thrust his hand out.

"I actually was the one that grabbed him first," said Meade. "But I only grabbed him to protect myself. I thought he was going to shut me off or bump me real hard. That's why I put my hand out to keep him off. I wasn't going to have him put me through the fence."

Riding racehorses was a rougher business in those days than it is now. With no patrol film available in 1933 for stewards to use in scrutinizing races for infractions, jockeys were known to do anything short of homicide to win, whether it was leglocking other riders, slamming opponents into the rail, whipping rival horses across the face, or grabbing the bridles, reins, or saddlecloths of any moving object within reach.

Fisher, no Boy Scout in jockey silks, didn't guide Head Play over to the inside just to tell Meade the way home. "I went in to tighten things up on Meade," said Fisher. "I could have throwed him if I'da shut him off completely. If I'da completely cut him off and he'da had to stand up and pull up, well, hell, there'da been nuthin' to it. I'da won off 2 or 3 lengths. But I didn't want to shut him off completely. His horse's legs might have hit my horse's back legs and caused a fall. I didn't want to do that, so I just tightened it up."

By reaching over and pushing Fisher, Meade was the first offender. Fisher would be the second.

"I pushed him off me to get running room," said Meade, "and then he took ahold of me. Now I'm not going to sit there and let him lead me down there to the finish line. I couldn't push him away from me because he had ahold of me so I had to get ahold of him. So from there down to the finish line that's what it was—we grabbed, grabbed, grabbed all through the stretch. It was the survival of the fittest. I couldn't sit there and let him rough me around and not do nuthin' about it. And, by the same token, he couldn't let me do anything that I wanted to do. He had to retaliate, too. Really, it was just a man-to-man thing that he couldn't help and I couldn't help. I'm not blaming him for trying to do what he did because in those days *that's* what you did. If you didn't do it, you wasn't a race rider."

Once things got out of control, there was no calling off the rough stuff, even if the tug-of-war would take place down the homestretch in view of the stewards. This was the Derby, *the* Kentucky Derby, and each boy was determined to get the better of the other.

"When I put him in tight quarters," said Fisher, "he reached over and grabbed my saddlecloth at the eighth pole and held onto me. I tried to shake him loose by squeezing him against the fence and he just held onto me. I was so amazed to think that he had the *nerve* to have ahold of me that I kinda lost my head. I blowed my top. I hit him across the head with my whip once or twice before the finish and then after the finish."

Fisher slashed Meade with his whip soon after the horses passed the finish line. But did Fisher hit Meade with his whip earlier in the race, as he said he did?

A story in 1933 said Meade charged Fisher with striking him twice with his whip. But Meade later recalled that Fisher hit him only after the finish. Maybe it was asking too much of these former jockeys to recall everything that took place in the heat of battle. As Meade told me years ago when I asked him whether Fisher had used the whip on him during or after the race—or both, "Oh, hell, my mind wasn't even on that. My mind was on winning the race. I didn't give a damn about that. A guy who's fighting, he don't even know when he gets hit, you know."

Head Play's left rein was slack in those final, fateful yards. "He switched from my saddlecloth to my left shoulder and almost pulled me off the horse," said Fisher. "That's what caused the reins to dangle like that. They was practically pulled out of my hands. For an eighth of a mile, my horse practically pulled two horses—hisself *and* Brokers Tip.

"I thought I rode the horse absolutely perfect until he grabbed my saddlecloth," Fisher added. "I don't think I could have rode a better race up until the last eighth of a mile, and then when he held onto my saddlecloth, there was too much confusion. I got maybe a little bit mixed up. I was greatly disappointed in myself . . . I figured that I had ridden the best horse and I had got beat on the best horse, and I had got outroughed—and I was pretty rough myself."

In a movie taken from high up at Churchill Downs showing the last part of that Derby, Meade can be seen whipping Brokers Tip (that was his *own* mount, remember) on the right side approaching the sixteenth pole. Meade didn't apply the whip again. Driving toward the finish, he held the reins snugly in his left hand and had the whip in his right hand. With that right hand, he reached over to grab at his opponent.

With about fifty yards to go, Fisher dropped his right hand, then recovered and pulled it back up, appearing to grab the mane of Head Play (nothing illegal there; Head Play was *his* horse). To this observer, Head Play held a slight lead inside the sixteenth pole, Brokers Tip then edged in front, but in the last stride or two Head Play appeared to make a final surge. Brokers Tip was ruled the winner, triumphing by no more than two or three inches, according to *The Blood-Horse* magazine.

But there was no photo-finish camera at Churchill Downs

in 1933, so how could anybody be certain who won such a close race? In fact, the movie, though certainly not conclusive, could lead a skeptic to wonder whether it was Head Play who actually won the race, a contention that Fisher made for years.

A person watching the movie can rerun the film time and again in an effort to examine the race for details, but back at the 1933 Derby, the thirty to forty thousand fans—that's right, no more showed up in that depression year—didn't have any instant replays or slow-motion reruns. The stretch duel happened, and, just like that, it was over.

It took Wally Lowry's photograph to preserve the action for newspaper readers the next morning . . . and for history.

Meade and Fisher were suspended thirty days each for their rough riding. The stewards slapped Fisher with an additional five-day suspension for attacking Meade afterward in the jockeys' room.

Lowry's photograph "brought on the action by the stewards to do something to both of the jockeys," Earl Ruby, retired sports editor of *The Courier-Journal,* believed. "That's the only thing that could have. Nobody else knew anything. If it hadn't been for that picture, nobody would have said a word."

Through the years, many tales and fairy tales would circulate about this photograph. The most far-fetched story is that Lowry was passed out drunk underneath the rail, happened to wake up during the stretch run of the Derby, snapped his picture, and promptly passed out again. Another account suggested that Lowry was assigned to take a Derby picture from a position across from the finish line near the outside fence but was "three sheets to the wind" in the infield when the race started. By the time he made his way over to the rail, the horses already had run once around the track and were at the head of the stretch. Lowry, thus trapped in the infield, decided to shoot from underneath the rail. And then there's the belief that Lowry was "drunker than a goat," just fell out from under the rail, took the photograph, didn't know what he had shot, and had to be carried back to the office.

There are other stories. For instance, because of Lowry's condition—you guessed it, he was drunk or hung over—the only reason he was under the rail was that was the most comfortable position in which to put his body: down on the ground. Or somebody bet Lowry that he wouldn't take a head-on picture from under the rail, so he merely accepted the challenge. Or he had no idea what he had taken and, after giving his glass plate (which was used instead of sheet film) to somebody else to be developed, he went to a bar.

Make no mistake. Lowry didn't have anything against taking a drink or two (or three or four or more, for that matter). "They always said he could set a camera down and reach for a bottle of whiskey and accidentally hit the shutter and make the damnedest picture you ever saw," recalled Charley Pence, who photographed for years for *The Courier-Journal* and *The Louisville Times.*

And I can't argue with the idea that Lowry didn't realize that he had taken a breathtaking picture.

But contrary to all the legends, Lowry's picture was a carefully planned assignment.

Clete Martin, a longtime racing fan from Louisville, recalled standing some ten feet away from Lowry when the picture was taken.

"He was down on his knees," said Martin, who was in charge of the infield security at the '33 Derby. "As they came down the stretch, this photographer rolled out on the track, snapped the picture, and rolled back."

Some years ago I mentioned the story about Lowry's alleged inebriated condition to Neil Dalton, the managing editor of *The Courier-Journal* in 1933.

After Dalton quit laughing, he said, "Ooohhh, no, hell, I'da kicked his teeth in if he'da been drunk."

Dalton went on to provide the background that led to this sensational photograph. "What happened was, oh, I guess about a year or two before, the *St. Louis Post-Dispatch* got a head-on picture of a race up there. Manny Levi, who was then the vice-president and ran the show, sent me the copy of the thing and said, 'Why can't we do something like this?' It was a beautiful picture, coming down head-on. The idea was here were some horses head-on with their feet off the ground. So we just took off—if they can do it, we can do it. So we did.

"Well, the next Derby, Charlie Betz, who was then the head photographer, and I worked on the thing, and we went out and determined how it would be possible to get a picture from the inside because at that time the track had very strict regulations that the photographers had to be on the grandstand side of the track and had to line up at an angle."

Dalton said that the plan for Lowry in 1932 was to wait until the Derby horses were getting into alignment for the start, and then, at the last possible moment with everybody's attention directed toward the head of the stretch for the beginning of the race, Lowry was to slip across the track and drop down on his stomach in the infield. Lowry wasn't to be concerned with the horses as they raced past him the first time. His only objective was to take a photograph of the finish. For Lowry, his 1932 picture turned out to be The Futile Photograph.

"Charlie Betz had given him directions on how to set it—the speed and all that kind of business—and he muffed it," said Dalton. "When the plate was developed, here it was, it just had missed—period."

Interestingly, at the 1932 Derby, a head-on homestretch photograph was taken by *The Courier-Journal*, but the cameraman was standing up. However, that picture, which was used in the paper the morning following the '32 Derby, didn't have the effect of a low-angle shot showing hoofs flying, and the next year the plan was repeated with Lowry.

Lowry had a helper with him, Wally Blair, a *Courier-Journal* correspondent who assisted with the photography equipment. Lowry again waited until right before the start, sneaked across the track, and got down in position. Unlike today's photographers, who can send a whole roll of film clicking through their cameras in a matter of seconds, Lowry didn't have the luxury of such sophisticated equipment. Using a bulky, old-fashioned camera, he had one shot—and one shot only—as Meade and Fisher struggled with each other in the driving finish.

Lowry's timing had to be perfect. He rolled out on the track and placed the camera down on the ground.

"It was just by the grace of God that he shot this one," said Dalton. "We were shooting for a head-on of the finish, and this other thing [the jockeys grappling with each other] was just a gift."

Not until the glass plate was processed at the rotogravure plant did anybody know what Lowry had photographed. Called into the darkroom, Lowry was told, "Look what we got."

"I saw this thing, and you wouldn't believe it," recalled Dalton. "It was a blowup. The thing knocked your head off."

Thornton Connell, who was the newspaper's political writer, was handling duties as photograph editor that particular night. "Lowry didn't know what he had," recalled George Koper, a Louisville newspaperman from 1928 to 1974. "Thornton told me they all jumped with joy just as soon as they saw the picture."

The picture, which appeared at the top of the page but with the spire cropped out, wasn't used in the early editions. "We recognized what we had—that it was pretty good—so we held it out and then hit with it," said Dalton. "It didn't go on the street until after midnight at least."

On the next morning, the following item on page 1 of *The Courier-Journal* alerted the readers to the picture: "A remarkable photograph of the Kentucky Derby finish appears on the front page of The Courier-Journal Rotogravure Section. It was taken by Wallace Lowry, staff photographer, from the ground under the inside rail as the horses were a few jumps from the finish line. This exclusive photograph shows the end of the race from an angle seen by no one but The Courier-Journal cameraman."

The Courier-Journal immediately copyrighted the photograph. "I remember very distinctly the Associated Press refused to pick up the picture because of the copyright," recalled John Herchenroeder, who was associated with the newspaper for more than fifty years. "They could have very easily carried it and said copyrighted by *The Courier-Journal,* but they wouldn't do it so they missed out on carrying that picture."

An Associated Press photographer standing near the outer fence shot the finish. His picture showed Fisher leaning over and interfering with Brokers Tip, but the view of Meade's right arm was blocked out just enough by Head Play to leave the readers wondering. As *The New York Times* stated: "It is not clear from the photograph what Meade is doing with his right arm."

It was certainly clear in Lowry's picture, which provided the only peek of what was going on between the two combatants.

Lowry undoubtedly prefocused on a spot where he decided to take the picture. Opinions differed among professional photographers as to whether Lowry was looking through his camera when he snapped the picture.

Billy Davis, who later served as chief of the newspaper's photography department, didn't believe that Lowry was. "He had his camera on the ground, set," said Davis. "And I'd say he had his left hand firmly planted on top of it so it wouldn't move and with his right hand he shot the picture. He wouldn't be looking through the camera. He's watching the horses, and when they hit that spot he was in focus for, he shot it."

Davis didn't think that Lowry was drunk. "He couldn't have been drunk and timed that that well. Your reflexes are not that sharp when you're drunk."

Luck, of course, played a big part in the picture. Lowry had to be in the right place at the right time, and the jockeys had to be fighting. Lowry took that luck and, combined with advance planning and his ability, pulled off a photographic gem.

Wallace Lowry. (Courtesy *The Courier-Journal*)

Lowry, who died in 1957 at the age of fifty-four, later went to work for the Associated Press. While with the AP in Pittsburgh, he went to the automobile races on an off day but had his trusty camera with him anyway. Two cars crashed right in front of him, and Lowry took a sensational picture of the wreck. That photograph was selected by the AP as one of the ten best pictures of the year.

But nothing he could ever shoot would surpass his Fighting Finish picture.

In 1983, Tom Hardin, head of the newspaper's photography department at the time, had this to say about the picture: "It's one of the great moments in the Derby, and it's been captured by Wallace Lowry. It's so graphic. It shows the arms out there in the middle; it reads so quickly. It shows the spire. It puts it in an unmistakable place. It's certainly dramatic in the rush of the horses. The hoofs are up.

"It's one of those memorable pictures that sticks in the mind. It's something that's frozen forever in the back of somebody's mind once they see it. It ranks with the pictures of other memorable events that people *always* remember, whether it's from the Vietnam War or from World War II or from the assassination of President Kennedy or the assassination of Robert Kennedy, certainly the assassination attempt of George Wallace. There are others—the Hindenburg fiery demise in New Jersey, the picture of Babe Ruth standing at home plate, shot from behind. You always remember those images."

Others who have spent their careers in professional photography have been overwhelming in their praise of this picture.

"God, I don't see how anybody could make a shot like that, even sitting still," Pence once said. "It's the best sports picture I've ever seen. It's a beautiful thing. We must have sold thousands of prints on that thing—every size you can think of. I must have printed 500 of them myself."

"I think it's a great picture," George Bailey, a former *C-J* photographer, recalled. "It's one of those once-in-a-lifetime things. It's the most meaningful sports picture I've ever seen."

The Courier-Journal has gotten plenty of mileage from the photograph. Bud Kamenish, another former photographer for the newspaper, recalled that the picture was used as a symbol for special Derby editions.

"At one time they used to send souvenir Derby editions around the world for about ten cents," said Kamenish, who sold those editions as a newsboy. "They had like a mailing cover that they wrapped it in to mail it, and they would take just the Derby edition part of the paper and then the mail room would wrap it with this souvenir cover and they had at the top 'Remember This'—and it was a picture of the Fighting Finish. That became their souvenir symbol."

While *The Courier-Journal* took great pride in the photograph, as Lowry did himself, Churchill Downs was embarrassed by the picture. The Downs, it seems, thought that this photograph reflected unfavorably on the sport's image.

The track refused to allow any such head-on finish photographs to be taken for years. Actually, photographers don't have any business doing what Lowry did, rolling out on the track. Horses obviously can be spooked.

The Downs now permits photographers to use remote-control cameras that are placed under the rail near the finish. Some outstanding photographs have been made by these motorized cameras, showing Derby winners approaching the finish with all four feet off the ground and the twin spires in the background. Yet none of these photographs measure up to what Wally Lowry took in 1933.

If Wally were alive today, he'd learn that his photograph has appeared in numerous books, including *A Century of Champions,* a publication by the Associated Press, which initially didn't send out the picture because of the copyright.

Not only that, but Wally would probably chuckle to find that Churchill Downs has recovered from its initial embarrassment and has decided to take advantage of the photograph. If Wally could go out to the Downs today, he couldn't help but notice the blown-up print of his photograph in the jockeys' room. He also would see the picture hanging in the press box, and he could find in the files a 1983 Kentucky Derby media guide with a front cover showing Louisvillian Johanna Hurst Veeneman's oil painting that was done off his famous photograph. Lowry would learn that eight-by-ten glossy prints—500 of them, altogether—were ordered from *The Courier-Journal* so that the Downs could provide them in press kits distributed to the media in 1983.

Lowry would see his own head shot included in a press-box memorial to those members of the media who have covered the Derby with distinction.

And if Lowry would go out on the track Derby Day and walk over to the finish line, he'd see all those remote-control cameras set up by photographers hoping to get a spectacular picture.

They can do all the hoping they want, but unless in the highly unlikely event two other jockeys engage in hand-to-hand combat coming down the stretch, those photographers will never duplicate the picture that Wally Lowry snapped on May 6, 1933.

Even so, ol' Wally probably would be the first person to drink to those photographers' efforts.

13

Presidents at the Derby

AIR FORCE ONE LANDED at Louisville's Standiford Field at 2:00 P.M., 3½ hours before post time for the 1969 Kentucky Derby, and climbing out of the four-engine jet were President Richard M. Nixon and his wife, Pat. They were heading for Churchill Downs, the second straight year they were in Louisville for the Derby. In 1968, they had seen Dancer's Image beat Forward Pass. Later that fall, Nixon had defeated Hubert Humphrey in the presidential race. Now, on May 3, 1969, the Nixons returned to another Derby.

In 1968, they had been Kentucky governor Louie B. Nunn's guests for the Derby. "At that time he committed if he was elected president that he would come to the 1969 Derby," Nunn once recalled.

Nixon was pictured following the 1968 Derby in a champagne victory toast with Governor and Mrs. Nunn, Churchill Downs president Wathen Knebelkamp and his wife, and Mr. Peter Fuller, owner of first-place finisher Dancer's Image, and his wife.

Mrs. Nixon, who wore a green, blue and white printed silk dress and jacket costume in 1968, came to the next year's Derby brightly clad in a yellow and white two-piece, flowered suit. The First Lady was presented with a bouquet of roses from Mrs. Nunn at Standiford Field. Nixon shook hands with crowds at the airport, and then it was off to the races. Hovering over the airport and the motorcade to the Downs was an army helicopter.

Joe Hirsch wrote in *Daily Racing Form:* "The arrival of President Richard Nixon was preceded by a fly-past of several military helicopters. Promptly at 2:38 P.M., a pair of long black limousines swung into the area behind the stands from an obscure service gate. Members of the Kentucky National Guard, linked arm-to-arm, cleared a path through the crowd for the cars, which halted under the clubhouse dining room. A loud cheer swept the crowd as Secret Service men jumped from the limousine, followed by a smiling and waving President. As the President was escorted to a waiting elevator, the 25 GOP governors entered the track via the same route as the President and proceeded to the $250,000 rooftop lounge built to accommodate the party of distinguished visitors."

Nixon's visit to the Derby was a big story, even making the front page of *The New York Times,* complete with a photograph of him waving to the crowd at the Downs.

"Security was tight" on Derby Day in 1969—"from the spires on down to the tulip beds and over in the barn area," *The Blood-Horse* magazine reported. "Secret Service men, whose serious mien was indistinguishable from that of the normal race track player, inconspicuously infiltrated Churchill Downs long before Richard Nixon became the first President of the United States to witness the Kentucky Derby. Louisville police, Kentucky state police, National Guard troops, Churchill Downs security guards, and Thoroughbred Racing Protective Bureau agents co-ordinated security efforts with walkie-talkies to insure protection, not only of the President, but of the Republican governors whose spring conference in Lexington was concluded the day before the Kentucky Derby."

The Courier-Journal reported: "Once inside the Downs, Mr. Nixon moved to a new enclosed VIP section, covered with thick green carpeting and jammed with Republican governors and congressional leaders of both parties. Away from the press and public, Mr. Nixon got down to serious business.

President Richard M. Nixon was on hand for the 1969 Kentucky Derby, the only time that a chief executive has attended the race while in office. (© 1969 Churchill Downs Incorporated/Kinetic Corporation)

He put down a bet, sampled a julep and began making the rounds of the tables."

The newspaper noted that whether or not Nixon "actually drank the julep" appeared "to be a closely guarded administration secret." Nixon was quoted as saying: "I'm going to savor this race, Kentucky style." His press secretary, Ronald Zeigler, a native of northern Kentucky, said, "You might say that's part of Kentucky's style."

Nixon appeared in the fifth-floor VIP box section at 3:29 P.M., and his arrival brought forth a roar of applause and cheering from thousands in the packed crowd below him. On a day that attracted the president and an outstanding Derby field, the historic race drew its first 100,000-plus crowd in history—106,333 turning out in ideal weather.

The Nixons watched the sixth race with California governor Ronald Reagan and his wife, Nancy. Also with them was Mrs. C. V. Whitney, wife of the famous horseman.

Later, on his way through a pressing crowd to Nunn's box, Nixon encountered Sen. Charles Percy of Illinois, and, according to a story in the *Sunday Herald-Leader* in Lexington, told him: "Majestic Prince. Put it on that. The California horse." The newspaper also reported that Nixon told Sens. Mike Mansfield and Everett M. Dirksen and their wives: "Majestic Prince. He's going to win."

Nixon watched the Derby from Nunn's box, and when the favored Majestic Prince edged Arts and Letters in a thrilling finish, the president shouted to Mrs. Dirksen, who was seated on his right: "He won, he won!"

Nixon left as soon as the race was over.

The following headline the next morning was a natural: "95th Derby: A Prince and a President."

At the time, readers of *The Courier-Journal* weren't certain whether Nixon had won or lost on the Derby. His press staff put out a statement that the president bet on "the California horse," which was assumed to mean the only California-bred horse in the race, Fleet Allied, who finished seventh. Later, however, Nixon was quoted as telling Senator Percy to bet on Majestic Prince. One military aide claimed that the president "just cheered" and hadn't bet at all.

In reply to a 1978 query, John V. Brennan, assistant to Nixon, said: "The bet was on Majestic Prince. It was not placed by President Nixon. Someone else placed the bet and gave the ticket to President Nixon."

LBJ Not Talkative to the Press

Nixon is the only chief executive to watch the Derby while in office, but future and past presidents have been on hand for the classic. Harry S. Truman reportedly attended the Derby, Bill Clinton went to the Derby as governor of Arkansas, and Lyndon B. Johnson, as a Texas senator, came to Churchill Downs in 1952.

The Courier-Journal reported that LBJ "was uncommunicative, except to say he wasn't backing Gushing Oil, generally thought to be the Texas favorite."

"Beyond that," Johnson said, "I'm not talking. This is my day off."

Also attending the 1952 Derby were Dwight Eisenhower's son, Maj. John Eisenhower, and his wife. "This is my first Derby, but we've begun to feel like Kentuckians," said Major Eisenhower, who had been stationed at Fort Knox since the previous August.

Derby a "Great" Event

In 1969, besides Nixon, two future presidents—Reagan and Gerald R. Ford—were on hand for the Derby.

No president has seen more runnings of the Derby than Ford. In a 1989 letter, he wrote: "The first Derby Betty and I attended was 1969, when Majestic Prince was the winner. As Republican Leader in the U.S. House of Representatives, I participated in the Republican Governors Conference in Lexington.

"Beginning in 1977, Betty and I attended most of the Derbys for the next 10 years. Annually, we were guests of our longtime, dear friend, John Galbreath. We would spend the weekend at Darby Dan Farm in Columbus, Ohio, and fly in for the Derby."

Genuine Risk was "our favorite Derby winner," Ford wrote. "Betty was dedicated to the filly, despite all the expert advice from the gentlemen bettors. Genuine Risk, a gallant filly, came through in a great race. Betty was ecstatic in her success and gave the rest of the Galbreath party a hard time.

"We've always been thrilled with the excitement of the Kentucky Derby," Ford added. "It is one of the great American sporting events."

In 1992, Ford said that he and Betty hadn't attended the past few Derbies. "We always watch the Derby on TV and have a little side bet," he said. "I usually lose."

Ford, Carter, and Bush at the '83 Derby

In 1983, on hand for the Derby were two past presidents—Ford and Jimmy Carter—and one future president, George Bush, who was the guest of horseman William S. Farish.

Carter, wife Rosalynn, and daughter Amy came to the Derby as the guests of Dale Sights and his wife, Margaret Ann. Sights, a member of the Kentucky State Racing Commission and chairman of Carter's 1976 and 1980 presidential campaigns in Kentucky, arranged for the Carters to stay in a condominium owned by fellow racing commissioner, Kentucky breeder Tom Gentry. On Derby Eve, the Carters spent the night in the condominium in Lexington's Radisson Hotel, and the next morning they went to Gentry's farm. Carter jogged that morning with Sights and Gentry and took a firsthand look at a breeding farm's operation.

"I won't tell you how far I jogged—we won't get into that," said Gentry, but he did add that Carter "was in pretty good shape."

It so happened that Gentry owned a horse, Flag Admiral, who was running in the fourth race on the Derby Day card at the Downs. Laffit Pincay, Jr., had been named to ride the colt but was unable to arrive in time for the race. So Gentry, ever the showman, had Carter accompany him to the jockeys' room, along with quite an entourage, to pick a rider for Flag Admiral.

"He went into the jocks' room and tickled those kids to death—and started talking all that Spanish," Gentry said.

Bobby Peck, the Downs clerk of scales, recalled that the jockeys did indeed get a big kick out of seeing Carter. A good many of the riders shook hands with him. "They were very honored to do it," Peck said. "Everybody really was glad to meet him. We were proud to have him."

Peck remembered that jockey Charlie Woods "ran back in the kitchen and bought some peanuts and came out and handed them to Mr. Carter."

Carter, who joined Gentry in the paddock before the race, helped cinch the girth on Flag Admiral, according to *Daily Racing Form.* "With Gentry's assistance, Carter gave 'orders' to jockey Jorge Velasquez and spoke several words in Spanish, a language in which he is fluent," the *Form* added.

Sights recalled that Carter told Velasquez how to ride Flag Admiral—"and the race worked out *exactly* the way he told him to ride it."

Flag Admiral won the one-mile allowance race by 7½ lengths as the 1.90-1 second choice. Afterward, the Carters and daughter Amy went on the track to be photographed in the winner's circle.

"The ESPN cable-TV network caught Mrs. Carter for a quick interview," Billy Reed reported in *The Courier-Journal.* "'If Jimmy had a good time giving instructions today,' she said, 'we might be back a whole lot.'"

It was understood the former president "had a small wager on Flag Admiral, a hunch bet since Mr. Carter served in the Navy as commander of a nuclear submarine," *Daily Racing Form* reported. "During the afternoon, President Carter commented on how much he enjoyed attending the Derby, and Mrs. Carter commented that it might be fun to participate in the sport."

When Flag Admiral ran again two weeks later in the Preakness, Carter was part owner of the colt. It was reported that, according to a private agreement between Gentry and Carter, the former president stipulated that any financial gain from his interest in Flag Admiral go to the Jimmy Carter Library in Atlanta.

Carter's part ownership of Flag Admiral created a good amount of publicity, but the colt was not a serious contender against the type of opposition he faced in the Preakness. As a 26-1 long shot, Flag Admiral finished tenth, beating two horses.

Flag Admiral raced just three times after the Preakness. He won an allowance race at Churchill Downs the next month, finished eighth in the Ohio Derby eleven days later, and then was eased March 31, 1984 at Santa Anita Park.

President Bush at the 1993 Derby

Bush attended the 1993 Derby with Churchill Downs board chairman William S. Farish, a longtime friend and horseman.

"Former President Bush switched horses on Derby day without profit," John Crittenden wrote in *The Palm Beach Post*. "Early in the day, Bush told Wayne Lukas he would bet on Personal Hope, who finished fourth. Later, he told Dan Dorfman, financial writer for *USA Today,* his bet was going in on Lukas' horse, Union City. The Lukas entry came in 15th."

Wrote Dorfman: "President Bush lost another race—several in fact. This time, it was a series of horse-racing bets at Churchill Downs in Louisville, at the 119th Kentucky Derby.

"I chatted with Bush just before the big race, and he told me he had been losing money all day long. But he wasn't perturbed, declaring, 'I'll make it all back in the Derby.' Alas, he didn't. Bush bet on Union City, a Secret Service agent said."

Of the former president's visit to the Derby, *The Courier-Journal* reported: "Bush breezed through the Skye Terrace pumping hands, soaking up applause and stopping outside the Stakes Room to chat with two buddies—Robert Strauss, his former ambassador to Moscow, and Arnold Scassi, the New York-based fashion designer who helps dress Bush's wife, Barbara. 'I was hoping that Barbara would be here with him today, but she stayed in Houston to finish the house,' Scassi said."

Virginia Kelley . . . an Ardent Racing Fan

Virginia Kelley, mother of President Bill Clinton, was a horse-racing fan who came to Louisville in the fall of 1992

Former president George Bush attended the 1993 Kentucky Derby. (Photo by Zeljko Cvijanovic)

and planned her inauguration gown, which was designed by jockey Pat Day's wife, Sheila, owner of The Rose Boutique and Salon in Crestwood, Ky. Mrs. Kelley, a good friend of the Days, attended the races two days at Churchill Downs and made the trophy presentation following the Cardinal Handicap on November 14.

Mrs. Kelley was taken to the recreation room in the jockeys' quarters. "Everybody went around and met her," said Peck, the clerk of scales.

"I was standing behind my desk," Peck added. "I had turned my ankle the day before, and I couldn't walk. So they opened the door out in the hall, and they said. 'This is Mr. Clinton's mother. Would you like to meet her?' I said, 'I'd love to come out there and meet you, but I can't walk.' She said, 'By golly, I can.' And she walked right to my desk and shook hands with me."

The Blood-Horse reported in its January 30, 1993 issue: "[Mrs. Kelley] had a good reason to miss Oaklawn Park's

Virginia Kelley, mother of President Bill Clinton, was a racing fan. In 1993, Pat Day presented her with an album of Jockey Star Cards on behalf of Oaklawn Park's jockey colony. (Photo by Les Beale)

meeting opener for the first time in years—she attended son Bill Clinton's inauguration. However, the First Mother didn't stay away from racing for long. Accompanied by journalists Bob Woodward and Jack Germond, Kelley visited Laurel Race Course three days later."

She was quoted as saying: "The racing is very much like Oaklawn. I'm enjoying the action."

The magazine added: "Kelley said she'll attend the Kentucky Derby and possibly the Preakness Stakes. Last year, she backed Lil E. Tee in the Derby. However, Kelley doesn't expect the president to accompany her to the Triple Crown. 'He's a little busier than I am,' she said."

Mrs. Kelley did attend the 1993 Derby, her second trip to the race. She saw her other Derby in 1958. "The first time she was far from her new perch on Millionaire's Row, where she is the guest of Gov. Brereton Jones," Jacalyn Carfagno wrote in the *Lexington Herald-Leader*. "'I was out in the infield then and having a wonderful time. I loved it,' she recalled. Kelley's passion for racing has not passed on to her elder son. 'He likes racing, and he likes the people, but Bill has always been tied to his office.'"

The Courier-Journal checked on her betting during the afternoon and reported: "Sitting with Kentucky Gov. Brereton Jones, she studied entries for the sixth race and shook her head. 'I'm down, way down,' President Clinton's mother said. 'But I never bet enough to hurt me.'"

Mrs. Kelley was pictured in one newspaper sharing a laugh on Derby Day with Nippy Carville, mother of Clinton political strategist James Carville, and in another publication standing next to former baseball star Pete Rose on Derby Eve.

Trainer D. Wayne Lukas recalls spending time with Mrs. Kelley at Oaklawn Park in Hot Springs, Ark., in 1992 after Clinton was elected president. "She had me over, and I shared the table with her at Oaklawn," Lukas said. "When I got up to leave, she said, 'Would you write a note to Bill on my program?' I said, 'I'd be glad to.' And I wrote, 'To Bill, 85 percent of the production in racehorses comes from the dam. Everything you accomplish in life, you owe to your mother.' I'll bet he got a kick out of that."

Lukas has at least two winner's circle presentation photographs at Oaklawn with Clinton in the picture. "Bill Clinton is in my picture of Althea winning the Arkansas Derby [in 1984]," Lukas said. "He's there—with long, dark hair."

Mrs. Kelley, who died on January 6, 1994 at the age of seventy, was a woman who clearly had been bitten by the racing bug. As she said on Derby Eve in 1993, "I love the people, and I love the horses. I love everything about the racetrack."

A Call from the President

In 1994, for apparently the first time in Derby history, a presidential call was made to Churchill Downs after the classic. The Downs' communcations department put out the following release on the call:

> President Bill Clinton, whose mother, the late Virginia Kelley, was a big fan of thoroughbred racing, phoned Churchill Downs late Saturday afternoon to offer his personal congratulations to the winning connections of Go for Gin.
>
> The President first talked to W.J. Condren, who offered to share a secret with the President.
>
> "I have to tell you this, partner Joe Cornacchia is a Republican," Condren said. "I told him that if we were fortunate enough to get a call from you today, I would have him tell you what a great job you are doing."
>
> This drew a chuckle from President Clinton, who noted that his mother was a big fan of 1991 Kentucky Derby winner Strike the Gold, who was also owned in partnership by Condren, Cornacchia and Giles Brophy.
>
> Cornacchia also issued an invitation for the President to come visit the colt at Pimlico when the colt tries for the Preakness.
>
> "You know, my mother really would have wanted to come to the Derby and I would have liked to, too, but I had work to do," President Clinton said. "But I might take you up on Baltimore."

Trainer Nick Zito was next to talk to the President and he said, "I think your mom was smiling down on us today. She was a great lady. I got the chance to meet her at the Preakness."

"I'm very happy for you, Nick," President Clinton said. "It was a great day for racing."

Clinton also offered his congratulations to jockey Chris McCarron.

McCarron also praised Clinton's mother. "You know she threw out the first pitch for the Don MacBeth Memorial softball game. She lived for racing."

The President had watched the race from the White House and commented on the rainy weather in Louisville.

"Yes, Mr. President," Zito said, "but the sun is shining now."

The idea for the presidential call stemmed from Joe Hirsch, executive columnist for *Daily Racing Form.* J. Brian McGrath, commissioner of the Thoroughbred Racing Associations, also played a role in the call, as did Churchill Downs president Tom Meeker and Kentucky governor Brereton C. Jones.

"This was really Joe Hirsch's idea—100 percent," McGrath explained. "Joe just happened to call me from Gulfstream and said, 'Gee, Brian, wouldn't it be nice if the president called the Derby winner?' To the best of Joe's knowledge, no president had ever called a Derby winner. I had an opportunity to discuss the idea with Tom Meeker, who also was supportive of it. Subsequently, I was down in Kentucky and visited with Governor Jones, and Governor Jones was thoughtful enough to raise the possibility with President Clinton, and the president was gracious enough to make that phone call, which we very much appreciate. My hat's off to Joe Hirsch for taking the initiative. It was thoughtful of Governor Jones to put in a call on our behalf, and we very much appreciate the fact that President Clinton would make a phone call to congratulate the Derby winner."

Quayle Went with The Shoe

In addition to presidents, vice-presidents have attended the Derby, as have men who have unsuccessfully run for the nation's highest office.

Former vice-president Dan Quayle saw his first Derby in 1981. At the time a U.S. senator from Indiana, Quayle shared a box with two Kentuckians—former U.S. senator Marlow Cook and Sen. Walter ("Dee") Huddleston. *The Courier-Journal* said that Quayle acknowledged that he wasn't much of a handicapper.

"Quayle said he was depending on Cook for advice on the horses, and said he picked Cure the Blues because [Bill] Shoemaker was overdue for a Derby win," the newspaper reported. "Cook allowed as how he didn't think that was much of a betting system."

In response to a letter, Quayle wrote on August 30, 1994: "I did bet on Cure the Blues and lost money. I have not returned to the Derby since 1981, though I thoroughly enjoyed it. There *are* similarities between the Derby and the Indianapolis 500. They're both huge events for Louisville and Indianapolis. However, the dress code at the Derby is more formal than the Indianapolis 500. I wouldn't change either event. Horses are more dependable than cars. Horses almost without exception finish the race. In Indianapolis, about one-third of the field finishes the race."

Charles Curtis a Former Jockey

In 1931, Vice-President Charles Curtis, a former jockey, presented the Derby's gold cup to Mrs. Payne Whitney, owner of the victorious Twenty Grand. "Mrs. Whitney," Curtis said, "it gives me great pleasure to present to you in behalf of Churchill Downs this cup, which you have won with your wonderful horse. You have an excellent horse, a fine jockey, and an excellent trainer. I want to thank this organization for keeping up the tradition of old Kentucky by the breeding of Thoroughbreds."

Curtis also attended the 1931 Preakness, which was run a week earlier than the Derby that year.

"Before Mr. Curtis began his political career he was a jockey of considerable ability and promise," reported *The Blood-Horse.* "The son of a Kansas pioneer and a mother who was one-quarter Kaw Indian, he was brought up on the Reservation by his Indian grandmother, Julie Poppin, daughter of the Kaw chief White Plume. He learned to ride before he was three years old. He began race riding at the age of eight, on small Western tracks, and continued in that profession until he was 16, when he gave it up in order to educate himself. On his face he carried, for the remainder of his life, the mark of a scar received in a racing accident."

The Thoroughbred Record reported that Curtis "never lost his love for horses and racing and never missed an opportunity to attend a race meeting when possible."

Curtis said he never wagered on the horses after he became vice-president.

"In 1875 and 1876, during my last years as a jockey, I rode a celebrated Kentucky horse named Tilden," Curtis once recalled. "This horse was a stake winner in Kentucky under another name, but his owners thought he had broken down and consequently Charlie Search was able to buy him for a moderate figure. He was renamed when he came to the West, and I rode him in something like fifty races during two years, never suffering a defeat."

Alben, Alfred, and Adlai

There have been other runnings of the Derby with presidential or vice-presidential flavors, including the 1933 renewal with James Roosevelt, son of President Franklin Roosevelt, on the presentation stand and Woodrow Wilson's widow among those in attendance. Merrill Dowden wrote in *The Courier-Journal* that the tall, smiling Roosevelt "said he never had a better time in his life."

Roosevelt said: "No, I didn't pick the winner [Brokers

Tip], but the winner was my second choice. And, believe me, I'm coming back."

In 1953, Kentuckian Alben W. Barkley, a former vice-president, attended the Churchill Downs classic, saying he hadn't been to the Derby since "way back before the war."

In 1937, Barkley was in the Derby party of Vice-President John Nance Garner. ". . . And don't say we told you," Thornton Connell wrote in *The Courier-Journal,* "but Mr. Garner bet on Dellor to win."

Dellor wound up seventh in the field of twenty.

Connell wrote that Garner was attending his first Derby—"and he didn't attempt to conceal the thrill he was getting out of it."

Said Garner: "It is a beautiful place, a beautiful day. Everything is splendid, nearly so good as it was in Washington when we opened the baseball season."

Also attending the 1937 Derby was Alfred M. Landon, the GOP candidate for president in 1936. He was with his daughter, Peggy Anne. "Landon told us what he expected to bet on in the Derby," Connell wrote. "It was Dellor. He said a cab driver gave them Dellor as a 'good thing' on their way to the track."

Illinois governor Adlai Stevenson (the Democratic candidate for president in 1952 and 1956) also knew his way to Louisville for the spectacle on the first Saturday in May.

At the 1949 Derby, Stevenson was pictured with fellow governors Earle Clements of Kentucky and Fuller Warren of Florida. *The Courier-Journal* reported: "Governor Stevenson had his $2 on Johns Joy 'because I don't like a horse who is so much of a favorite.'" Johns Joy, a 15-1 shot, finished ninth.

At the 1950 Derby, Stevenson was photographed sitting between Basil Brooke, prime minister of Northern Ireland, and his wife, Lady Cynthia Brooke.

1907 Derby a "Good Party"

And then there were the Derby appearances of Alice

Roosevelt Longworth, daughter of President Theodore Roosevelt. In 1939, *The Courier-Journal* made a brief mention of her at the Derby, saying that she "occupied her usual box."

But back in 1907, when her father was president, the twenty-three-year-old Mrs. Longworth was big news at Derby time. On the day of the race, *The Louisville Times* ran this headline: "President's Daughter to see Kentucky Classic Run." The Longworths were the guests of former Cincinnati mayor Julius Fleischmann. "The Longworth party arrived at The Seelbach Hotel at 9:45 o'clock last night, four hours behind schedule time, drenched with rain, bespattered with mud, laden with luggage, tired and cold and hungry," the newspaper reported. "But even at that price, according to members of the party, they had gotten their money's worth in seeing the far-famed Bluegrass region and they were ecstatic in their expressions of pleasure in their visit through Central Kentucky. A large crowd had assembled at The Seelbach in anticipation of their coming and to get a glimpse of Mrs. Longworth. A ruse which she adopted, however, fooled most of the crowd. Mrs. Longworth entered the hotel in company with Mr. Fleischmann and she passed practically unnoticed to the elevator almost before it was known that she was in the hotel. Mr. Longworth and other members of the party reached the hotel in another automobile."

The day after the Derby, a photograph of Mrs. Longworth and her husband appeared on the front page of *The Louisville Herald.* A story elsewhere in the newspaper said that the Longworths "seemed to thoroughly enjoy the scene spread before them, and talked and laughed with the guests in their box as though they were not at all times the cynosure of all eyes."

The Courier-Journal headlined one story, "How the President's Daughter Saw the Thirty-third Kentucky Derby," and a heading over another story said: "Society Out in Bib and Tucker—Attention Divided Between the Derby and the President's Daughter."

The Longworths and others in their party "occupied a box

at the end of the grand stand, near the clubhouse, which was most considerate of them, as it was the best possible place they could have taken to let the crowd look," *The Courier-Journal* reported. "Or, to be strictly truthful, the crowd did not look, but just plain rubbered to its heart's content. And Mrs. Longworth did not take the trouble to return the gaze, but sat still and showed great repose of manner.

"Her much-advertised vivacity was not in evidence, and she did not give evidence of undue excitement or thrills when the Derby was run. It must be an awful thing to be a President's daughter and not be able to draw a natural breath without an extra being published about it."

Mrs. Longworth wore "a tasteful, simple gown of some soft, clinging, brownish material with an ecru lace blouse with a sloping fichu effect over the shoulders," the article continued. "Her hat was a small affair on the toque order, with shaded brown plumes at one side. Her toilette was completed by a golden brown boa of malines. The only thing out of the ordinary about the lady's appearance was the earrings of pearl that swung from her ears. They were long and in their shape suggested what our colored mammies used to designate as ear-bobs."

Of the earrings, the newspaper added: "It was good of the lady to wear them, as they were the only bizarre touch about an otherwise strictly conventional toilette, and it gave the women a good point to take hold of in their comments. Nobody seemed to like them very much, and everybody thought she would have looked better without them.

"One woman nearly wept because Mrs. Longworth's hair was not red, as had been reported. The comfortable, warm shade of brown of her hair was not enough to satisfy this disappointed woman."

One person described as "a jealous woman" was quoted as saying: "She doesn't look any better than anyone else. It's just her name."

Of 1907 Derby winner Pink Star, Mrs. Longworth said to her husband, "Isn't he sweet?"

In 1977, she was asked by Jean Howerton Coady of *The Courier-Journal* if she remembered what she wore at the 1907 Derby.

"Oh, heavens no!" she replied.

Mrs. Longworth, then ninety-three, said she didn't remember anything about the 1907 Derby except that it was "a good party."

Majestic Prince (middle) scored a neck victory over Arts and Letters (on the rail) in the thrilling 1969 Kentucky Derby. Dike finished a half-length back in third. (© 1969 Churchill Downs Incorporated/Kinetic Corporation)

14

My Favorite Derby

COL. MATT J. WINN HIMSELF couldn't have dreamed up a better Kentucky Derby than the 1969 renewal.

Colonel Winn, a master promoter for years as a Churchill Downs executive, was a great one for exaggerating the attendance, and in time it became traditional for the Derby crowd to be estimated at more than 100,000. Well, in 1969, it happened for the first time—106,333 turning out in favorable weather.

Included in the crowd was President Richard M. Nixon, the first chief executive to witness the Derby while in office.

Besides a huge crowd, good weather, and the appearance of the president of the United States, the ninety-fifth Derby had something that appeals to all racing fans—an outstanding field of horses. Majestic Prince, unbeaten in seven starts, was favored over such contenders as Top Knight, Arts and Letters, and Dike. All came through with strong efforts except for Top Knight, who wasn't right physically. Clearly, he wasn't the same horse who had whipped Arts and Letters by 2 lengths in the Flamingo and by 5 lengths in the Florida Derby earlier in the season.

Of the thirty-five Derbies that I've seen, this one had the smallest field—eight starters—and yet it stands out in my mind as the most memorable. It just goes to show, I guess, that bigger isn't always better.

Another three-year-old who raced at Churchill Downs that spring was Ack Ack, winner of the Derby Trial in track-record time. But he didn't run for the roses. Ack Ack went on to win the Horse of the Year title in 1971, an honor that Arts and Letters captured in 1969.

I've never seen a Derby that caused people to debate the merits of the various horses as vehemently as they did in 1969. Majestic Prince and Arts and Letters especially had their strongly opinionated backers, and for years you could start an argument by asking whether Majestic Prince or Arts and Letters was the better horse. (My opinion? Flip a coin, and I wouldn't quarrel if it came up in favor of Majestic Prince.)

I always liked Majestic Prince. I saw him auctioned off for a world-record $250,000 as a yearling, and I was on hand when he arrived at Churchill Downs with his trainer, Johnny Longden.

A handsome horse, Majestic Prince had a regal air about him, giving off the impression that he knew he was a good horse. This colt never raced again after a second-place finish in the Belmont Stakes, and I only regret that he didn't have a full career so that we could have learned just how good he really was.

When Majestic Prince came to the Downs that spring after a flight from California, a welcoming committee of seventeen admirers, including track president Wathen Knebelkamp, was on hand. The winter-book favorite for the Derby was an impressive-looking animal as he walked down the ramp from his van and strolled around the barn prior to being bedded down in stall No. 2 of Barn 39. A bouncy gait . . . an alert look . . . a bright, chestnut coat . . . a powerful frame (he stood 16.1 hands and weighed 1,120 pounds). Add all of that together and you had the winner of any equine body-beautiful contest.

"That's some horse," Knebelkamp said. "He's a real runner."

Mike Bao, assistant trainer, had his own way of describing

Majestic Prince. "He's a freak," Bao said. "He's as human as you'll get in a horse."

The weather-beaten Longden treated Majestic Prince like a little child. Indeed, that relationship between man and animal was not ordinary. Exactly how many trainers have you seen rub noses with a horse? It happened in Barn 39 the day that Majestic Prince arrived in ol' Kentucky.

A week before the Derby, I watched in awe as Majestic Prince won the seven-furlong Stepping Stone Purse in 1:21 $\frac{3}{5}$, just a fifth of a second off the track record. He led through six furlongs of that race in 1:09, which was faster than the Downs' eight-year-old track record of 1:09$\frac{1}{5}$.

Dave Whited, who rode Texas Dancer in the three-horse Stepping Stone and finished a full 21 lengths behind the winner, said of Majestic Prince: "I think he's a super horse. He does everything so easy."

The Stepping Stone led to a *Daily Racing Form* column that put Longden in a bad mood the morning before the Derby. The article, written in Baltimore, quoted trainer Bryan Webb as saying Majestic Prince would be the Derby's "biggest bustout since Silky Sullivan."

The article said that Longden made a strategic blunder in the Stepping Stone. Majestic Prince won that race in fast time and continued on to work out the Derby distance of a mile and one-quarter.

According to Webb, such an undertaking was far too much to ask of a horse so close to the Derby.

"I maintain that this was a suicidal move that even a super horse can't overcome," Webb was quoted as saying. "The damage has been done."

To which the irked Longden replied: "A man's got a right to his own opinion, but you don't go around belittling somebody else's horse. He doesn't even know what he's talking about."

What about the accusation that Majestic Prince "left his Kentucky Derby on the track" in the Stepping Stone? "Hell, no, he didn't," Longden shot back. "He just galloped out in that race. We've never really asked this horse to run. He doesn't know how fast he can run. This horse is something special."

Bao, the outspoken assistant trainer, had this to say leading up to the Derby: "We came to run. They ducked us last week [in the Stepping Stone], but they can't duck us now. Don't ever, don't *ever,* condemn a horse with all those ones behind his name. No matter who he beat, this horse is unbeaten.

"He'll give his best in the Derby, and he'll win it. I'll guarantee you that."

Joe Namath couldn't have put it any better.

Majestic Prince won the Derby in a thrilling stretch battle, defeating Arts and Letters by a neck. Dike, the Claiborne Farm colt who had my money on his nose, was a half-length back in third.

My assignment for *The Courier-Journal & Times* was to interview the winning jockey, who turned out to be none other than Bill Hartack. Hartack always seemed to be at his best in the Derby, but he wasn't always in the best of moods with the press, and that afternoon after he won the Derby he was something to behold. I'll never forget walking alongside him back through the paddock and going up the escalator to the jockeys' room after the race.

Keep in mind that Hartack had just won his fifth Derby, tying him for the record with Eddie Arcaro. Yet, after the race, on his way to the jockeys' quarters, he was besieged by numerous well-wishers and to one person who met him with a hard handshake, all he could say was, "I'm not excited. You guys are excited—I'm not."

Staring straight ahead, Hartack marched into the jockeys' room after the Derby and was greeted by a radio man, who poked a microphone at him and asked: "What's next as far as your career is concerned?"

"I don't know," Hartack said.

Hartack then sat down on a bench as valet Bob Powell helped him off with his boots.

Some fifteen newsmen, cautiously reserved, watched Hartack pull off the black-and-gold silks of owner Frank McMahon. Not a question was asked while Hartack undressed.

The silence appeared humorous to other jockeys, who showed by the looks on their faces that they were enjoying the situation.

Hartack was soon ready for his shower. He grabbed a towel and started to leave his would-be interviewers.

Finally, a question.

"Bill, did he break the way you wanted him to?"

No answer.

A photographer took a picture of Hartack as he finished showering. Hartack didn't mind this particular invasion of privacy—until the photographer asked, innocently: "Was it an easy ride?"

"That sounds like a question," Hartack replied perceptively.

"No, I'm just wondering for my own personal interest," the photographer explained.

"Sorry," Hartack said, "but I'm just so leery of newspapermen that I can't tell you."

Returning to his locker after the shower, Hartack was greeted by this daring question from a reporter:

"Who won the race?"

"Who knows?" Hartack said. Then, Hartack said what he had said so many times in the previous two years. "I'll be very happy to entertain any appointments for an interview. There won't be a mass interview."

"Okay," someone said.

"Can I have an interview in the next ten seconds?"

"No," Hartack shot back. "I have a right to refuse you. . . . Call me at my motel if you want an interview. But don't call me tonight."

"What about Sunday?" someone asked.

"If I make it through tonight," the jockey replied.

Another question: "Are you happy with the win, Bill?"

"You can't understand what I'm saying, can you?" the jockey said.

All the while, Hartack was dressing into his street clothes—beige pants, white shirt, black silk jacket, black shoes, black and white silk scarf.

Later, Hartack did grant a special interview to a friend, turf writer Russ Harris, in the jockeys' lounge.

Although Hartack didn't get along with virtually all reporters, that didn't mean he was friendless at the racetrack—not by a long shot. In the jockeys' room, there were several close acquaintances congratulating him.

After the Derby, most of Hartack's warmth was directed at two pals, valet Chuck Corolla and George Stidham, who was referred to as the jockey's business manager. As Corolla helped lead Majestic Prince into the winner's circle, Hartack reached down and playfully slapped the valet on his head. Later, Hartack embraced Stidham on the track.

But newspapermen?

"I've put up with newspapermen," Hartack said. "Now they've got to put up with me. If you guys start treating jocks like men, then maybe we'll start treating you like men."

That final burst ended the "interview," and most of the reporters left the room.

"Thank you, Mr. President," somebody cracked.

15

Calumet Farm: One of a Kind

CALUMET FARM HAS such a rich history and such a proud tradition that it will forever be remembered for its postcard beauty, the white fences and the rolling green pastures . . . for its many great runners, Citation, Whirlaway, and others . . . and for all the gold and glory that it earned on the first Saturday in May at Churchill Downs—eight Derby trophies, a number that most likely will never be matched by another stable.

No other farm has produced so many genuine stars, so many Hall of Fame runners. Calumet's tradition and heritage are forever woven into the sport's history.

This is the farm that stood for the *finest* in horses, having bred nine Kentucky Derby winners, the first—Whirlaway—in 1941 and the ninth—Strike the Gold—fifty years later.

In the 1940s and 1950s, Calumet Farm built a racing dynasty that no doubt will never be equaled again. Since then, Calumet has enjoyed a degree of success, but it took on a different approach in 1982 after the death of Calumet owner Lucille Parker Markey. The farm was inherited by daughter-in-law Bertha Wright (beneficiary of a trust that was the majority owner of Calumet) and her children.

J. T. Lundy, a son-in-law of Bertha Wright, became president of Calumet, and under his direction the farm spent millions, including huge expenditures for stallions. (Where did you go, Mogambo?) In the fall of 1990, Calumet suffered a major blow with the untimely death of Alydar.

Lundy resigned as Calumet president on April 3, 1991, and was replaced by Lexington horseman John T. Ward. On March 26, 1992, Calumet was purchased by Henryk de Kwiatkowski. De Kwiatkowski successfully bid $17 million to acquire Calumet's principal spread of 762 acres. He also successfully bid $210,000 for Calumet's name and $175,000 for a 33-acre plot at the back of the farm.

"When I heard this wonderful farm was being threatened, it was a personal offense to me," he said. "I want to assure all of you—all of my new neighbors—that not one blade of grass will be changed. The farm will be maintained just as it is for as long as I live, and I hope my children and their children will maintain it after I'm gone. It is the crowning achievement of my life that I now own it."

In its heyday, Calumet was unique in the truest sense of the word—one of a kind. Even though most of Calumet's success took place in the 1940s and 1950s, the farm later rose back to prominence under the training of John Veitch. In 1976, Veitch took over as Calumet trainer, remaining there until he resigned in 1982. "The first year was very dry," Veitch once said, "but all the rest were good years for me and Calumet."

They were good years, indeed. Veitch trained Alydar, runner-up in all three Triple Crown races in 1978, and three champion fillies for Calumet—Our Mims, Davona Dale, and Before Dawn.

However, the great years took place in the 1940s and 1950s, a time during which Calumet Farm boasted the most powerful dynasty in the sport's history.

What was it like? What brought about the Calumet greatness?

Well, we talked with four people who played major roles in

the Calumet story—the trainer who worked for the farm for almost a quarter of a century and sent out two of the stable's record eight Kentucky Derby winners, two employees who spent a total of more than eighty years there at the farm, and the jockey who rode three of Calumet's Derby winners.

First, a quick refresher course on Calumet's history.

In 1931, three years after his family sold its interest in the $40 million Calumet Baking Powder Co., Warren Wright, Sr., converted Calumet Farm from a trotting horse to a Thoroughbred nursery when he inherited the Lexington establishment from his father, William Monroe Wright.

Wright gradually built his Calumet dynasty. In its first year at the track, 1932, Calumet accomplished very little, winning but one race. However, in three years' time, the stable was strong enough to send out the Kentucky Derby favorite, Nellie Flag. Then, in 1936, Wright made the soundest invest-

Mr. and Mrs. Warren Wright, Sr., at Saratoga in 1940. (Courtesy Keeneland-Cook)

ment of his life, purchasing a yearling for $14,000 at Saratoga. The horse, Bull Lea, who ran an undistinguished eighth in the 1938 Kentucky Derby, earned $94,825 in his career for Calumet. He was a fine racehorse, certainly a credit to Calumet, but his real value came at stud when he served as the backbone of the farm's breeding operation.

In 1939, Wright made another acquisition that was to strengthen Calumet immensely. He hired Benjamin Allyn Jones, better known as Plain Ben, as his trainer. Jones, who had saddled 1938 Derby winner Lawrin, was just the man Wright needed to get Calumet's devil red and blue silks steamrolling ahead.

Jones' son, Jimmy, assisted him in those early years and later became Calumet's trainer. Both of the Jones Boys would wind up in racing's Hall of Fame, as would eleven Calumet horses, nine of whom they trained.

Jimmy trained Citation, though his father went into the record books as having won the 1948 Derby with that colt, and sent out back-to-back Derby winners in Iron Liege (1957) and Tim Tam (1958).

When Jones left Calumet Farm in 1964 (three years after his father had died), he had trained more winners (thirty) of $100,000-added races than any horseman in the sport's history. According to Jones, a lot of sweat and the right kind of blood helped establish the greatness of Calumet.

"Everybody was working and doing the best they could," Jones said. "Everybody kinda had their shoulder to the wheel a little bit and pushing as hard as they could push. And then we were fortunate to have the blood. Raised some good horses and got the best out of them. Bull Lea turned a lot of it in, and then the Blenheims and the Bull Leas seemed to cross awfully well. Bull Lea had a good disposition, which the Blenheims needed badly. The Blenheims had good legs, quite a lot of ability, but they needed to settle their nerves down a little bit. Bull Lea did that."

Bull Lea ranked as America's leading sire for five years (1947-49 and 1952-53) and sired three Derby winners for

Calumet—Citation, Hill Gail (1952), and Iron Liege.

As successful as Bull Lea was at stud, his sons were disappointments as stallions. In 1968, Henry Forrest, who trained Forward Pass, the eighth Calumet horse to bring home a Derby trophy, was quite candid in his assessment of the farm's problems after its two-decade dominance. "The bottom of Calumet fell out when Bull Lea started going downhill as a sire and they didn't find somebody to replace him," Forrest said. "They should have shot Citation long ago. He's never been anything as a stallion.

"Their breeding became stale. They kept breeding their mares to their own stallions. Lately, they've started breeding to outside stallions more, bringing in new bloodlines. It's helping Calumet a lot."

Even though Citation didn't achieve much at stud, he was quite a racehorse. To be sure, Jones calls Citation the greatest racehorse he has ever seen. "I never saw anything he couldn't do when he was in his prime—before he got hurt," Jones said.

Citation compiled a record of twenty-seven wins in twenty-nine starts in his first two seasons of racing (1947-48), then missed his prime four-year-old campaign after developing an osselet. "After he got hurt, that's a different thing," Jones said. "But before he got hurt, he could do anything. He could outrun the sprinters, he could outrun the two-milers, he could outrun the mud horses, and he could outrun 'em on a dry track. I didn't let him win way off and try to break world records unless he was *forced* into it. I was trying to preserve him for *another* race. If you don't use them too hard, you're there for another day. He could do everything. I've seen horses that were great on a fast racetrack, but when they got mud, then they weren't great anymore. They got to be able to do everything really good to be great, in my opinion, and that's the reason I always thought Citation was better than any of the rest of them."

Citation became the first millionaire in racing history, retiring during the 1951 season with earnings of $1,085,760.

Wright didn't live to see Citation reach the $1-million mark. He died December 28, 1950.

Jones described Wright as a businessman, not a horseman. "He didn't know anything about horses, but he apparently had the Midas touch for doing business. Everything he touched turned to money."

His widow, Lucille, married Gene Markey on September 27, 1952. "She was interested in racing until she got remarried. She was *deadly* interested in it up till then, and I think she was going to make a pretty good owner. But after she got married, why, then she was madly in love with this guy. And he was a nice guy, too. But he didn't understand racing. She was a little too conservative to buy any more horses. The blood was running out. She had a lot of money, but she wouldn't buy anything. I think she was over-economical. Mr. Wright was economic enough, but he *would* buy a horse."

Jones said that Wright didn't like any "red ink" on the ledger sheet. "It was important to us to be in the black," he said. "We were in the black, you know, twenty-four of twenty-five years."

Calumet was the country's leading money-winning owner for twelve years (1941, 1943, 1944, 1946-49, 1952, 1956-58, and 1961). In 1947, the farm piled up earnings of $1,402,436, the first time an owner had gone over the million-dollar mark in a single year. Calumet won more than $1 million in each of five other years (1948, 1949, 1952, 1956, and 1957). No other owner would top $1 million until 1960, and Calumet's earnings record of $1,402,436 would stand up until 1969.

The forties were particularly big years for Calumet. During that decade, the farm raced five Horses of the Year—Whirlaway (1941, 1942), Twilight Tear (1944), Armed (1947), Citation (1948), and Coaltown (1949, in one poll).

The stable became so powerful that it was split into divisions, with Jimmy taking a group of horses to California. "They'd get in each other's road if you didn't do that," he said. Calumet was the leading money-winning owner at Hollywood Park from 1951 through 1954.

Margaret Glass came on board at Calumet Farm on April

29, 1940. "I always said I got in on the front-row seat of what was going to happen because that was Whirlaway's two-year-old year—and that's when things began to click," said Mrs. Glass, who managed the business end of things for virtually all of her 42½ years at Calumet. Whirlaway, a long-tailed, temperamental son of Blenheim II, won the Triple Crown in 1941, and seven years later Citation would provide Calumet with its second sweep of these three coveted races.

Mrs. Glass could write a book about her experiences at Calumet. (But don't bet that she ever will. Still loyal to the Calumet that she once knew and loved, she'll always bleed devil red and blue.) A walking encyclopedia about Calumet during its glory years, she can recall in detail how it was to work for Wright.

"Mr. Wright was strictly a businessman," she said. "He was fair. He *would* get mad. When he got mad, he would get red up in the top of his head, and his hair was thinning white and you could see the red in the top of his head, we used to say. But he would say what he had to say and he would get through with it and the next thing you knew he was turning around talking about something that was mutually agreeable and pleasant. It was very seldom that he ever got mad at me—maybe two or three times that I can even think of over a difference of opinion. One time I told him what I was thinking about some subject, and he said, 'Oh, you're crazy.' I said, 'No, Mr. Wright, I may be wrong, but I'm not crazy.'

"So that ended that conversation, and in about, oh, a matter of minutes, he was on some other pleasant conversation in a chatty way as if we had never had these words exchanged. And I *resented* that. Of course, I was quite young. And then it dawned on me that that's the best lesson you could ever learn from anybody: say what you've got to say, get through with the subject, *change* the subject into something mutually agreeable, and *go on*. Don't pout, don't hold grudges, move on. And that's what Mr. Wright taught me. That's the best lesson he ever taught me, and it bespeaks the man.

"There are a lot of people who ask advice from people and then they don't take it. Mr. Wright was smart enough to pick out the people who knew, or should know, and he took their advice. Now that's where he beat some of the rest of them."

Mrs. Glass talked about the differences in Wright and his wife, later Mrs. Markey. "Mr. Wright believed in paying right, but Mrs. Markey was tight. She didn't believe in paying people overly—by any means. And if it hadn't been for the charisma and the admiration and the love and the close-knit feeling of the employees as to being a part of what we called 'The Calumet Family,' we wouldn't have stayed. There was something about that place that we felt was top-notch and special."

Mrs. Glass will always have a fond place in her heart for Alydar.

"Alydar was my favorite horse," she said. "For one thing, he extended Mrs. Markey's life for the best part of five years. She was—my word for it was 'resurrected.' I mean, she was really failing, and that horse, with his charisma, well, it just woke her up—that's what kept her going for the best part of five years. Alydar did it—there's no two ways about that in my mind."

Alydar's gallant second-place finish to Affirmed in the Belmont Stakes is a race that sticks out vividly in Mrs. Glass's memory. "It was one of the outstanding races of horsedom," said Mrs. Glass, who watched the race on television from Lexington. "I seldom cry, but that's the only horse race I ever cried over in my life. The tears just rolled down my face. So he was a special horse to me."

Mrs. Glass said two letters that she received from breeders maybe ten to fifteen years before she left Calumet in 1982 best exemplified what the farm stood for. One breeder, a doctor from South Carolina, "said he liked to breed with us because of our considerate ways, sense of humor, and impeccable reputation," Mrs. Glass recalled. "Another breeder from out west said he liked to breed with us because of our honesty, dedication, and that we were the ultimate in class.

"If people are trying to get the feel of how it used to be, how better to describe how it used to be? I'm telling you that

Alydar, with Jorge Velasquez up, paraded to the post for the 1978 Blue Grass Stakes. (Courtesy Keeneland Association)

Calumet owner Mrs. Gene Markey (white hair) and her husband (far right) watched Alydar in the post parade for the 1978 Blue Grass Stakes. This race was the last one that the Markeys saw in person. (Courtesy Keeneland Association)

that's the way it used to be. That says it in six little phrases."

Hall of Fame jockey Eddie Arcaro used just one word to describe the Calumet dynasty: depth.

"Calumet had such depth," said Arcaro, who rode Whirlaway, Citation, and Hill Gail to their Derby victories for Calumet. "Like when Ben Jones was training, when one would break down, he had two on the bench that could beat the one that broke down. I rode Hill Gail in the Derby, and he come out of the race bad. That night I was with Ben Jones. I said, 'I really feel bad about that. That horse could have gone on and won the Preakness and could have won more.' He said, 'Eddie, I got one in the barn that could pull a cart and beat him.' It was Mark-Ye-Well. He always had somebody on the bench."

Like Hill Gail, Mark-Ye-Well was by Bull Lea out of a Blenheim II mare. Where Hill Gail didn't race again at age three following the first Saturday in May, Mark-Ye-Well won four stakes in 1952—the Arlington Classic, Clang Handicap, American Derby, and Lawrence Realization—and all four came after the Kentucky Derby. For the year, Mark-Ye-Well compiled a record of 7-2-2 from eleven starts and bankrolled $268,745, compared with $226,725 for Hill Gail.

In the year-end voting by Triangle Publications Inc., publisher of *Daily Racing Form* and *The American Racing Manual,* Mark-Ye-Well finished third for best three-year-old male and Hill Gail was fourth. In The Blood-Horse Handicap, Frank E. Kilroe assigned Mark-Ye-Well 127 pounds, 1 below Hill Gail and 3 below champion One Count.

Another example of Calumet's bench strength came at the 1957 Derby when Gen. Duke, the winter-book favorite, defected on the morning of the race, and the farm was left with Iron Liege. All he did was beat the best field of horses ever to run for the roses, including Gallant Man, Round Table, and Bold Ruler, Hall of Famers all.

Arcaro rode many of Calumet's best horses at the track, horses who had been broken back at the farm by Ewell Rice.

Rice worked at Calumet more than forty years, mainly with

Alydar charged to a 13¼-length victory in the Blue Grass Stakes. (Courtesy Keeneland Association)

Alydar following his victory in the Blue Grass Stakes. (Courtesy Keeneland Association)

yearlings. He broke Citation, Coaltown, Armed, and other great ones in those early years and later supervised the breaking of many more outstanding runners, including Tim Tam, Our Mims, Alydar, and Before Dawn.

"It was a first-class operation—very best of everything," Rice said of Calumet during its heyday.

Rice is working at another first-class operation these days—Claiborne Farm, near Paris, Ky.

The veteran horseman doesn't expect to see another Calumet dynasty. "That is something that probably only comes around once in a lifetime," he said. "Now it could come around maybe the next century or something like that, but I don't think any one farm or one outfit is going to dominate it like Calumet did at one time."

Calumet Farm . . . it was one of a kind.

16

That Temperamental Mr. Longtail

THE SPRING, SUMMER, AND FALL of 1941 were months of restlessness and uncertainty for the American people, many of whom believed the United States would be drawn into World War II. Even so, Americans tried their best to enjoy themselves at sporting events during that year. In baseball, fans watched Ted Williams hit .406 for the Boston Red Sox, the last time a major-leaguer has reached that plateau. And in Thoroughbred racing, the public's heart was captured by a sensational chestnut colt with a long tail. His name was Whirlaway.

Whirlaway was talented, but temperamental—exciting, but erratic. He could throw in a devastating three-eighths of a mile kick, but he also could throw in the towel. It took just the right combination—the training expertise of B. A. ("Plain Ben") Jones and the riding skills of Eddie Arcaro—to get winning results from Whirlaway in the 1941 Triple Crown races. The Calumet Farm star was voted Horse of the Year that season and the following year as well.

Whirlaway was born April 2, 1938, coming from the first American-sired crop of Blenheim II, the Aga Khan's 1930

Whirlaway, with Johnny Longden up, was known as "Mr. Longtail." (Courtesy Keeneland-Cook)

Epsom Derby winner whose offspring were noted for their soundness of body but not of mind. Blenheim II was syndicated and brought to America in 1936. Calumet owner Warren Wright, Sr., purchased a quarter interest in the stallion. It was said that the British trainers didn't want anything more to do with Blenheim's offspring, who were unpredictable and so difficult to handle. His sons and daughters weren't any better behaved in the United States, though they did have ability. One of his daughters, Jane Gail, was an extremely fast filly, but the Jones Boys—Ben and his son, Jimmy—never could get her tamed down. Jane Gail failed to distinguish herself in eight career starts, but in retirement she produced Hill Gail, the 1952 Kentucky Derby winner who inherited some of her crazy tendencies.

As for Whirlaway, he demonstrated his ability—and his idiosyncrasies—in the very first start of his career. He won a five-furlong race at Lincoln Fields in 1940, doing so even though he bore out badly coming into the homestretch and ran down the lane on the far outside. Whirlaway also was a problem horse in the paddock as a youngster.

Something had to be done, and Plain Ben was the man to do it. The willful Whirlaway became his private pupil. Whirlaway was just a two-year-old, and his ability was evident. But it would take hours and hours of work in order to straighten him out. If Ben could correct Whirlaway's bad habits, the effort would be well spent. If he couldn't, it would be a tremendous waste of time and talent.

The Jones Boys ran an organized, precise operation at Calumet, and each morning the stable would send out its horses in sets. One set would go out to the track in orderly fashion, then return to the barn. Then another set would go out, like clockwork. Besides the work on the track, there were chores back at the barn—cooling out horses, washing them down, cleaning the tack. Meanwhile, Plain Ben would be off on his own with Whirlaway. Ben devoted his complete attention to this colt, schooling him in the paddock, teaching him to stand calmly in the starting gate, taking him to a grassy area to graze, returning to the paddock.

Jimmy Jones has never forgotten the hours and hours of work that his father put in with Whirlaway. "He just took that horse and wore him down, just wore him down," Jimmy said. "He'd be gone two or three hours. Whirlaway was a *bastard* in the paddock. So we just went to the paddock with him every day. He stood in there and stood in there until he got so he was the best horse you ever saw in the paddock.

"That was one of the greatest jobs of training I ever saw, really. Whirlaway just seemed to have a knack of doing the wrong thing until you straightened it out. He was a peculiar horse in that he had a very stubborn disposition, but he learned and he would respond to habit building—and that's really what made the horse go. He was a horse that you had to put the habits in his head. He had to believe that was the only way to do it."

Whirlaway certainly was capable of some strange antics on the racetrack. "There are some turfgoers who believe that Whirly's supreme race was the Saratoga Special when he was a 2-year-old," Arthur Daley once wrote in *The New York Times*. "That was when he was at his knuckleheaded worst. He was running so hard that he never did make the turn but ran straight into the outside rail. By the time Johnny Longden got him unwound Mr. Longtail was an absolute last. Did he win? Don't be silly. Of course, he won. He came like the whirlwind he was to triumph in the very last twenty-five yards."

Actually, it's not clear whether Whirlaway went to the outside fence on his own volition in the Saratoga Special or whether, for some reason, he was ridden in that direction. The footnotes in the *Daily Racing Form's* chart said that Whirlaway was "steered to the extreme outside rounding the stretch turn and finished with a cyclonic rush . . ." Another chart, this one from the Associated Press, said Whirlaway "was taken to the outside and, going wide entering the stretch, closed fast to win going away." Almost going down after being jammed in close quarters soon after the Special's start, he was last among the eight starters in the early going. He moved up to fourth or fifth at the stretch call, a full 6 to 7½ lengths behind the leader, and somehow made up the ground at the end to win the six-furlong sprint in an amazing effort. He triumphed by a length or a length and a half.

In his two final starts before the 1941 Kentucky Derby, Whirlaway reverted to his old habit of running wide turning for home. Ridden by Wendell Eads, Whirlaway bore out on the stretch turn in the Blue Grass Stakes at Keeneland and, five days later, in the Derby Trial at Churchill Downs. He finished second in the two races, both times as the odds-on favorite. Our Boots won the Blue Grass by 6 lengths, and Blue Pair triumphed by ¾ of a length in the Trial.

Eads, just seventeen years old at the time, recalled nearly half a century later that he simply wasn't strong enough to keep Whirlaway under control. "I was so small that I couldn't hold him," Eads said. "I only weighed about one hundred pounds then. He was just too much horse for me. He'd run out on the turn and lose so much ground. I couldn't keep him from running out."

Whirlaway had been kept quite busy in his juvenile season and in his three-year-old campaign leading up to the Derby, starting twenty-three times altogether before the first Saturday in May of 1941. A game of musical riders had been played on his back, with seven different jockeys having been given a leg up on the colt. Longden, a future Hall of Famer, had been aboard Whirlaway in ten of his races, all in 1940.

Eads had ridden Whirlaway in two of the colt's starts, both victories, in 1941 before the losing efforts in the Blue Grass and Derby Trial. Quite concerned over Eads' unsatisfactory rides in those two races, Ben Jones put out a call for Arcaro, the Master himself. The elder Jones had won the first of his record six Derbies in 1938 with Lawrin, who was ridden by Arcaro.

Arcaro, who was under contract to Greentree Stable and had never ridden the wild Whirlaway, wasn't particularly eager to accept the assignment. "I didn't want to ride him, really, because I had seen too many good riders that couldn't handle him," Arcaro once recalled. "I didn't know why I thought *I* could handle him. They were having a lot of trouble with him. He would bolt."

Joan Payson, the daughter of Greentree owner Mrs. Payne Whitney, asked Arcaro to do her a favor.

"What is that?" Arcaro asked.

"Go ride Whirlaway," she replied.

"But I don't want to ride him," Arcaro said.

"Well, you're doing me a favor," said Mrs. Payson. "I owe Mrs. Wright a favor."

So Arcaro reluctantly headed to Kentucky to ride Whirlaway.

Arriving in Louisville two days before the Derby, Arcaro said, "I've never sat on the horse. But I believe he's a good one and has as good a chance as any of them to win if ridden right."

Jones, who knew Arcaro didn't want to ride the colt, told the jockey: "Well, I know you've heard so many stories about him, but you know I wouldn't send for you if I didn't think that I could correct it. This is the fastest horse in America right now, and with you riding him, we'll win the Derby."

Having Arcaro on hand to control Whirlaway was a big plus. Another was a one-eyed blinker. Jones followed Jimmy's suggestion of equipping Whirlaway with the one-eyed blinker, which had a cup covering the outside eye so as to make Whirlaway afraid to run out where he couldn't see. With Arcaro in the saddle, Whirlaway wore that one-eyed blinker in a workout on Derby Eve, and the fearless Jones positioned himself on a pony five or six feet out from the inner rail at the head of the Churchill Downs homestretch. The idea was for Whirlaway to hum around the corner and then hug the rail as he charged between the fence and the pony on which Jones was seated.

"I just said to myself, 'If the old man is game enough to stand right there, I guess I'm game enough to run him down,'" Arcaro recalled. "Ben Jones never moved a muscle, and Whirlaway slipped through the narrow opening as pretty as you please. I'll tell you that son of a bitch was flying, too. If he had ever hit Ben Jones, neither one of us would have been around to talk about it."

Whirlaway worked a half-mile in fifty seconds or so. With the lesson learned and Arcaro now sharing Jones' confidence, Whirlaway was ready for the Derby. Even though he had failed as the heavy favorite in his last two races, the public hadn't lost faith in him, sending him off as the Derby's betting choice, though it was at a tepid 2.90-1. As an old black cleaning lady at Calumet Farm replied after a houseguest asked why Whirlaway had lost the Blue Grass to Our Boots, "I don't know why he *wouldn't* run, mistuh. All I know is that he *kin* run."

Such celebrities as Lana Turner, Tony Martin, Don Ameche, Patricia Morrison, Andy Devine, Joe E. Brown,

Charles Butterworth, and Robert Young were among the Derby Day gathering. The crowd was treated to one of the greatest individual performances in Derby history.

Arcaro, the complete jockey, took hold of Whirlaway early in the race and kept the colt moving along in just a high gallop. Swinging into the clubhouse turn, he was eighth in the field of eleven. When Arcaro called on him to run rounding the far turn, Whirlaway took off like a bolt of lightning. Arcaro recalled, "A clocker told me after the race, 'That horse did something I never ever seen a horse do—or thought a horse could do. He run an eighth of a mile in just a little over ten seconds.'

"Just turning for home, I couldn't hold him," Arcaro added. "He was running all over the top of horses. I got him in high gear—now I couldn't hold him."

Whirlaway, fourth after a mile, flew down the stretch, his long, thick tail streaming behind him. He sizzled the final quarter in $23\frac{3}{5}$ seconds, just a bit slower than Secretariat's remarkable effort in the 1973 Derby—slightly faster than :$23\frac{1}{5}$. Soon after crossing the finish line, Arcaro looked back over his right shoulder. His nearest opponent was a full 8 lengths back. The margin was impressive, and so was the time: 2:$01\frac{2}{5}$ for the mile and a quarter, a record that stood until 1962, formerly the longest that a track mark held up in Derby history.

"He was the runningest son of a bitch I ever sat on," Arcaro said in the jockeys' room afterward. "I wouldn't say the best, but the runningest."

Years later, Eads looked back on that Derby and said: "I think I could have win on him if I rode him that day. See, that's the first time they run in that one-eyed blinker. I didn't have so much trouble with him after they put the one-eyed blinker on him."

A week after the Derby, Whirlaway captured the Preakness, the second jewel in the Triple Crown, in similar come-from-behind fashion, charging from last in the field of eight to win by $5\frac{1}{2}$ lengths.

By the time the Belmont rolled around, Whirlaway faced

only three opponents. The only hope for the opposition, it seemed, was that a slow pace might work against Whirlaway. "I knew they were in a plot against him—of course, you would know that," Arcaro said. "I told my wife going to the racetrack that day, 'If they don't run the first half-mile better than 49 seconds, I'm gonna let him go to the front. I can't hold him slower than that.'" Itabo led the field through the first half-mile in 49⅘ seconds, and Arcaro, turning to the other two riders in the race, said, "The hell with this, fellas, I'm leaving." Arcaro, seizing the initiative, proceeded to move to the lead with Whirlaway, opening up an advantage of at least 7 lengths.

"But I want to tell you something, he was a drunk dude," Arcaro said. "I could have outrun him from about the eighth pole home."

The wobbly Whirlaway won by 2½ lengths, becoming the fifth Triple Crown king.

"He was just a mixed-up kid, really," Arcaro said. "He got so much better after that."

Even though he won the Triple Crown and the Horse of the Year titles in 1941 and 1942, captured twenty-two stakes, was inducted into racing's Hall of Fame, and was the first horse to win more than half-a-million dollars ($561,161), Whirly had holes in him. His biggest hole, it seems, was his heart. If challenged, he was known to call it quits.

Charles Hatton, the late *Daily Racing Form* columnist, once wrote of this champion: "Whirlaway never really cared to be a racehorse. We never thought he had too much heart, as he would try to run out into the parking lot if a horse hooked him."

Arcaro and Jimmy Jones refuse to put the stamp of greatness on Whirlaway.

"I don't think any horse is great that has the idiosyncrasies he had," Arcaro said.

"Whirlaway had several things lacking in him," said Jones. "He was not dead game. If a horse would run with him a ways, he could kinda knock him out a little bit. He had a tendency to give up."

Longtime racing steward Keene Daingerfield also referred to Whirlaway's lack of heart. "I must say that Whirlaway was not one of my favorite horses," Daingerfield observed. "While his best races were terrific, he always impressed me as resembling a one-punch fighter. If he hit his opponent with his Sunday and he didn't go down, Mr. Longtail might resign; as he did when Our Boots beat him in the Blue Grass."

Following his four-year racing career, Whirlaway went to stud at Calumet. In 1950, he was leased for three years to French textile magnate Marcel Boussac and was shipped to Europe to stand at Haras Fresnay-le-Buffard, in southern Normandy. Boussac later negotiated an outright purchase of the stallion. On April 6, 1953, Whirlaway died suddenly. He was fifteen, the youngest age for any Triple Crown winner to die. Altogether, Whirlaway sired eighteen stakes winners, among them Scattered, who captured the 1948 Coaching Club American Oaks. Many of his offspring had his catchy name incorporated in theirs, including Whirl Some, Whirl Flower, Whirling Fox, Whirling Bat, and Risk a Whirl.

Whirlaway's legacy, however, was not as a sire. Beloved by a legion of fans, he will always be remembered as a classic-winning racehorse—"Mr. Longtail," the wild horse with the tremendous kick.

Exterminator, with Albert Johnson in the saddle, is shown at the Independence Handicap on July 4, 1922. He finished sixth under 140 pounds, the heaviest impost of his career. (Courtesy Keeneland-Cook)

As for Sun Briar, he was bred in France, and he had a legion of followers coming into the Derby. On Tuesday of Derby Week, the morning of Sun Briar's workout at the Downs, railbirds lined the track to watch the big colt, but what they saw was far from spectacular. Accompanied by trial horse Exterminator in the first half of the workout and by another stablemate, Nelsweep, in the second half, Sun Briar failed to distinguish himself, covering the Derby distance in 2:12⅘ on a muddy track.

The Derby outlook was anything but sunny for Sun Briar.

According to one story, Kilmer told McDaniel not to run Sun Briar in the Derby unless he could guarantee that the colt would triumph. "If I could guarantee the horse would win, I would run a three-horse parlay and have more money than you do and wouldn't have to be bothered with you anymore," declared McDaniel, who would be one of eight trainers to condition Exterminator in the seven years (1918-24) that he raced for Kilmer.

Although Sun Briar's name would remain listed in the prospective field in the Louisville newspapers up to a day or so before the Derby, he wasn't destined to make it to the post. He wasn't right and hadn't trained satisfactorily in his most recent works. The heartbroken Kilmer withdrew the colt from the race. Many people felt sorry for Kilmer. Even the *Daily Racing Form* sympathized with him in a Derby Day editorial expressing regret over Sun Briar's misfortune. Readers of the *Form* also learned that Kilmer would be represented in the Derby by another horse—Exterminator, a rank outsider who hadn't started in 9½ months.

Following heavy morning rains on Derby Day, the weather began to clear by 1:00 P.M., and the crowd, including many soldiers, packed the Downs. Evidence of the U.S. involvement in World War I could be seen at the track. War taxes on tickets had raised the admission prices from $2 to $2.20 for men and from $1.50 to $1.65 for women. There was a War Savings Stamp Booth, and it was doing a brisk business.

Readers of *The New York Times* woke up to this headline

on the morning of the race: "Only One Eastern Entrant in Derby." That Eastern representative was War Cloud.

"One reason for the paucity of Eastern candidates is that the Preakness Stakes, which will be run at Pimlico next Wednesday, will carry $15,000, the same amount given for the Derby," *The New York Times* reported. "This has kept Papp, Jack Hare, Jr., the Whitney candidates and others in the East, and accounts for the small field of ten in the classic."

The story pointed out in the second paragraph that Sun Briar wouldn't be running in the Derby, but no mention was made of Exterminator until the last paragraph, which carried a list of all of the entrants. The one brief mention of Exterminator did manage to spell his name correctly, but, of all things, J. C. Milam (who had sold the three-year-old to Kilmer) was listed as his owner and the reference labeled the gelding as a "c," as in colt.

"Though lacking in quantity, there will be quality in the field as Escoba gained a meritorious victory over Papp in the Breeders' Futurity at the end of last season," *The New York Times* added in its story. "This son of Broomstick was under a cloud last week because he was beaten in his first race. He redeemed himself on Monday, however, by winning the Derby Preliminary, and beating many of those he will have to meet tomorrow.

"War Cloud, considered the chief competitor of Escoba, has not been seen in public this season. He has been carefully prepared by Trainer Jennings, and on Monday last ran a sensational trial over the full Derby distance of a mile and a quarter, which he covered in 2:05 2-5. This is said to be the fastest trial ever run by a Derby candidate, and far better than has been credited to any of the other competitors. James T. Clark also had a good workout when he covered the distance in 2:08 2-5 and finished well within himself.

"There is the usual interest in the running of the classic, and a tremendous crowd is expected at Churchill Downs when the gates are thrown open for the opening of the New Louisville Jockey Club, which will last for fifteen days."

The Derby attracted a crowd estimated at between thirty thousand and fifty thousand. (Yes, there was that wide a variance in the news accounts.) The rainy morning was reported by *The New York Times* to have kept "many thousands" away from the track, but *The Louisville Herald* reported: "Altho the elements were particularly ungracious for the big day, the great expanses of the Downs were choked as never before." *The Thoroughbred Record* reported the gathering as "the greatest crowd that ever thronged Churchill Downs" and later in the story as "one of the largest crowds in the history of the organization."

The magazine added: "By the records of hotels and the statement of people who keep tab on such things there was probably a wider representation of the country in the throng than on any previous Derby Day. There were people here, it was said by the management, from nearly every state in the Union. Also, there were men from Canada, France and England.

"As the horses came from the paddock onto the track in parade to the post for the opening race, the band struck up the national anthem, and at the same time the stars and stripes were run up to the top of the tall flag mast in the center field. Everyone stood—the soliders, who had come in goodly numbers from Camp Zachary Taylor, at attention, and the male civilians, with their heads uncovered. Two of the jockeys, Frank Murphy and Lee Mink, took off their caps when they heard the strains of 'The Star Spangled Banner,' and saw 'Old Glory,' floating to the breeze, a resplendent guarantee to the freedom of the nation and earnest evidence that our fighting forces and their allies will make the world safe for democracy. And just at the moment of the good old flag's ascendancy the sun shone out from behind the vanishing clouds until it was bright enough to cast shadows from the trees and shrubs upon the lawn. While the band was playing the national air Governor and Mrs. A.O. Stanley arrived. They occupied a box set apart for them."

One place spectators didn't flock to on Derby Day was the

track's infield. In a Derby Eve story, *The Louisville Herald* reported that Downs general manager Matt Winn "announced that it had been deemed inadvisable this year to carry out the custom of former years and throw open the centerfield to all desiring to witness the Derby. This, however, does not mean that this time-honored custom has been abolished. There will be free admission to the grounds to those not desiring or unable to pay the usual charge. Such persons can enter by the Fourth street gate and will find plenty of room in the space surrounding the track proper and on the stable grounds."

It seems that in the spring of 1918, with the country experiencing a potato shortage, that crop was planted in the Downs infield. One thousand bushels were auctioned off, and the money was donated to the Red Cross. Potatoes weren't the only things grown in the infield that spring. *The Louisville Herald* reported in its coverage of the Derby: "One strange sight met the eye—over in the infield where customarily thousands are wont to gather as the privileged and untaxed guests of the club, there waved instead the unbroken green of growing rye, a deference to war demands and a tribute to Uncle Sam. However, the gay army which abounds in laughter and jest and which looks on annually from the 'free field,' fared well at other surreptitious vantage points, where they were not disturbed, while other unnumbered hundreds 'dug up the price' and came in thru the main gates to mingle with the grandstand throngs."

Another means of raising money came after the Derby when a small dog was auctioned for the benefit of the Red Cross. Thomas Carney of St. Louis purchased the dog for $700.

The Courier-Journal provided this description of the betting scene: "Before the Derby was run the pavilion was a mass of civilians, soldiers, both black and white. . . . At the beginning of the third race the crowd gained in proportions, and it became almost impossible to move from one machine to the other. The anxious spectators who couldn't find room to walk on the concrete floor had no hesitancy in using other people's feet, but as fast as they came up and flashed their greenbacks they were given a ticket."

War Cloud, in his first start of the year, was sent off as the Derby favorite at 1.45-1. Other horses with wartime names included Rifle in the first race, Lance in the second, and Counterblast in the third. "The popularity of horses bearing military names was noticeable," *The Courier-Journal* pointed out. "Hundreds of officers and enlisted men from Camp Zachary Taylor flocked to the sheds and intermingled with the masses of civilians."

Maj. Gen. Harry C. Hale, commander of the Lincoln Division, witnessed the Derby from the judges' stand as the guest of Charles F. Grainger, president of Churchill Downs.

An unprecedented development at the 1918 Derby was the appearance of women in the betting shed. In the past, the women relied on husbands, boyfriends or messengers to run their bets down to the windows, but in 1918, at a time when women throughout the country were crusading for their right to stand in the voting lines, dozens of women were standing right there with the men in the betting lines. Messengers were still being used by some women, several of whom were victimized on Derby Day by men who ran off with their betting money after presenting themselves as official bet carriers.

Those people who wagered on jockey Danny Connelly came out ahead for the afternoon. He won with five of his mounts on Derby Day—Regalo, Bradley's Choice, Fruit Cake, Mack Garner, and Manokin. In his only other ride that afternoon, he finished second aboard Sedan.

When the Derby rolled around, Kilmer and his wife made sentimental bets on Exterminator, their "ugly duckling" whose past performances showed nothing more than two insignificant triumphs in four starts as a two-year-old. A field of eight went to the post, with outsiders Aurum and Jim Heffering withdrawn after having been entered.

At the rise of the web barrier, the filly Viva America shot

to the front and led the field around the clubhouse turn and on down the backstretch. War Cloud was in the middle of the pack, while Exterminator, of all horses, began to gain. Near the far turn, the big, bony gelding moved through on the rail.

Receiving a ground-saving ride from the accomplished Knapp, the surprising Exterminator rushed into the lead and then faced a challenge from Escoba at the top of the stretch. Midway down the stretch, Escoba managed to edge in front, but Exterminator overtook him and sloshed to a stunning upset victory. Exterminator, the pinch runner, won by a length over Escoba, who tired in the final furlong. It was another 8 lengths back to the 29-1 shot Viva America in third.

"Viva America ran a wonderful race in the tough going for a filly," said her trainer, W. N. Potts. "She tired during the final furlong but held on gamely just the same. She is a wonderful filly and will win many a race around the Kentucky tracks this season."

Viva America, a daughter of McGee, won the Kentucky Oaks—the three-year-old filly counterpart to the Derby—on the final day of the Downs' 1918 spring meeting.

War Cloud, who finished fourth in the Derby, went on to become the first horse in history to run in all three Triple Crown races. He won a division of the Preakness and finished second in the Belmont.

American Eagle, ridden by Earl Sande, finished last, and twenty-six years later another Derby starter by that same name also would bring up the rear in the Churchill Downs classic.

"Though all the Winter long Mr. Kilmer had been credited with holding the trump card for this blue ribbon event in Sun Briar, the two-year-old champion of last year, his victory with Exterminator came as a complete surprise to the large crowd," reported *The New York Times*. "Experts had agreed that the only chance for an Eastern success was through the medium of War Cloud, and the chances of the home turfmen were considered brighter when the rain changed the condition of the track so that it was not to the liking of the Macomber imported champion."

Exterminator's payoff in the Derby was a whopping $61.20 straight, a return that at that time in Derby history ranked second only to Donerail's $184.90 payoff in 1913 as the race's highest win mutuel. Interestingly, Exterminator and Donerail both were sired by McGee.

"I have always thought that I would ride the Derby winner since Mr. Kilmer shipped his stable to Louisville, but I never dreamed that Exterminator would be my mount," said Knapp. "I had counted on riding Sun Briar and had that colt started he would have won the race without the question of a doubt.

"Exterminator ran a game race," Knapp added. "I always had something up my sleeve, and when I made my move he responded with great courage. I followed riding instructions to the letter and am glad that I met with no mishaps. Right after his last workout with Sun Briar, Mr. McDaniel said that he believed he would win the Derby, and when he threw me up on him today he told me to hurry home as I was on the best horse, even if a whole lot of people did not believe the same way he did."

McDaniel was quoted as saying: "After Exterminator beat Sun Briar so handily in his trials I realized that he was a good colt, making due allowance for the fact that Sun Briar was not near his best form. When I entered him in the Derby, I thought he stood a good chance, but knowing that he was racing against the crack three-year-olds in America I did not consider him a certainty by any means. I always thought, however, that he stood an excellent chance."

Keep in mind that this was the same McDaniel who reportedly didn't bet a nickel on Exterminator in the Derby but had his money instead on War Cloud.

McDaniel may have lost his bet, but he and Knapp reportedly were each presented with a $1,000 check from Kilmer for Exterminator's Derby victory. In addition, the stable's employees were told that their wages for the month of May would be doubled.

The thunderstruck Kilmer had this to say after the Derby:

"Gee, but it is great to win a Derby. I am delighted that I purchased Exterminator. He is sure a great horse, and he can have anything in Binghamton."

Kilmer should have been telling everybody just how lucky he was. Because if he hadn't accepted some advice or if it hadn't been for a tardy train, Kilmer would never have run Exterminator in the Derby. History is unclear as to the exact events surrounding the final decision to enter Exterminator in the Derby. One story has it that Kilmer's wife persuaded him to run the horse. Another gives Churchill Downs' Matt Winn credit for advising Kilmer to put Exterminator in the race.

And according to another tale, Exterminator would never have raced in the Derby if a train had arrived on time. After Sun Briar was withdrawn from the Derby, it seems that Kilmer decided to ship his horses back to New York immediately to join up with the main stable. The Kilmer horses were all ready to return to the East, but the railroad car failed to show up near the Downs at its scheduled time on the Thursday night before the Derby. When the train still hadn't appeared by nine o'clock Friday morning, Kilmer decided that since he couldn't get away from the Downs, he might as well run Exterminator in the Derby.

Further underlining just how lucky Kilmer was to win the roses was the fact that when he purchased Exterminator from Lexington turfman J. Cal Milam, he had no idea that the horse was even nominated to the Derby. Exterminator, who was foaled May 30, 1915, had been acquired by Milam at a Saratoga yearling sale. Although legend had it that Exterminator was an unattractive yearling with no promise and an uninspiring pedigree, Milam said otherwise. He said he acquired Exterminator because "he was right good looking and he was well bred and I got him at what I considered a cheap price." The price: $1,500.

Milam made a nice profit on reselling Exterminator to Kilmer, but the exact amount of that transaction isn't certain. The day after the Derby, newspaper readers in Louisville would have had every reason to scratch their heads in trying to learn what Kilmer paid for Exterminator. *The Courier-Journal* declared that the price was $15,000. *The Louisville Evening Post* noted that although the price had been reported at $15,000, it actually was $10,000, of which $9,000 was cash and $1,000 was made up by two colts valued at $500 each.

McDaniel later was reported to have said that the price was $9,000, plus two maiden fillies valued at $500 each. Still another source stated that the price was as low as $7,500, while another put it at $12,000.

Whatever it was, after the transaction, certain newspapers intimated that Kilmer planned to run Exterminator in the Derby, a suggestion that the owner vigorously denied.

Kilmer refuted that story with these comments for the press: "In view of certain misleading press reports regarding my purchase of Exterminator, I desire to say that I did not acquire this horse as a Derby candidate, but on the contrary as a trial horse for Sun Briar, with the idea of helping my Sundridge colt in his preliminary work for the Derby. In fact at the time of purchase I did not know Exterminator was eligible for the Derby. Buying Exterminator was in accordance with instructions to my trainer issued months ago and is a well-established part of my plan in getting Sun Briar ready for the great classic event. Those familiar with my stable affairs know that I have been looking a long time for a gelding that would go well enough to make Sun Briar extend himself in the trial work, and I believe Exterminator embodies everything I wanted in such a horse. It is also equally well understood that I do not consider Exterminator in the same class with Sun Briar. For these reasons I want to correct the impression that Exterminator was purchased by me as a prospective Derby winner."

People reading those comments might have been wondering if it was the same Kilmer who, the day after the big race, was quoted in *The Courier-Journal* as saying that when Sun Briar and Nelsweep (yes, he reportedly also considered running that three-year-old in the Derby) showed him that they weren't ready for the classic, "I then scurried about to get a worthy representative for the Derby, the price being of secondary consideration, and when I happened upon Exterminator I surely made a lucky strike. Sun Briar made a name for himself as a 2-year-old and he fell heir to Sun Briar Court at my place at Binghamton, N.Y., on account of his good showing, and Exterminator is right in line with him when it comes to my estimation of the two horses."

Exterminator and Sun Briar met twice in pre-Derby workouts, and here again stories differ on exactly which horse ran faster in the trials.

Later, Kilmer often would say that "Sun Briar could beat Exterminator doing anything," but guess which horse did enough to earn a place in racing's Hall of Fame? Exterminator, of course.

Exterminator, who later became known as "Old Bones," went on to prove that his Derby victory was not a fluke. In a career that spanned eight years, he won 50 of 100 races. He won at distances of 5½ furlongs to 2¼ miles. In thirteen starts beyond a mile and a half, he lost only twice.

A locomotive on legs if there ever was one, he hauled more than six tons of weight—12,580½ pounds—in his career. In 1922, a year that he was the best racehorse in America, Exterminator averaged carrying 132.7 pounds per start (2,256 pounds for seventeen races). He packed the highest weight of his career in a 1922 race, finishing sixth with 140 pounds in the 1½-mile Independence Handicap at Latonia.

At about the time of the Independence Handicap, *Lexington Herald* sports editor Joe Estes wrote what he later referred to as "a silly little ditty" that went along these lines:

There was a camel
  Whose back was broke.
One sprig of straw
  Made the poor beast croak.
It's a dang good thing
  For them that gamble

Exterminator
  Ain't no camel.

It was in 1922 that Exterminator won with the most weight of his career—138 pounds in the 1¼-mile Kentucky Handicap at Churchill Downs. In that race, his final appearance at the Downs, he went off at odds of forty-five cents on the dollar in a field of four. Ridden by Albert Johnson, the seven-year-old Exterminator triumphed by a length and a half. "When the celebrated McGee gelding passed under the wire he received a tremendous ovation, and it lasted for several minutes," reported *The Courier-Journal.* "It broke out anew with greater force than ever when Johnson brought him back to the judges' stand to weigh out. There never was a more popular horse locally than the Kilmer representative and he gains in the esteem of racegoers in this section every time that he performs here."

That race turned out to be Exterminator's last outing at Churchill Downs, where he made six starts altogether and finished in the money each time—four victories, one second, and one third.

During his career, Exterminator raced a total of almost 125 miles in his 100 starts.

"The people loved him," Estes once wrote in *The Blood-Horse* magazine. "As he was somewhat angular in appearance, they called him Old Bones, or Old Slim. Despite the high weights he carried and the stiff competition he met, and despite the fact that he was kept in training two years beyond his 7-year-old prime, they made him favorite in 62 of the 98 starts in which there was betting—and collected their bets 38 times in the 62. They passed around among themselves the stories of him, not only of his class and courage, but of how smart he was, and what a good 'shipper.' He had become a folk-hero when he was finally retired from the tracks and pensioned."

David Alexander wrote of Exterminator: "He was an even-tempered horse and seemed almost human at times. At the post, if he were next to a fractious actor, he'd simply lean against him and hold him until the tape was sprung."

Elaborating on Exterminator's "human qualities," Alexander wrote: "Even in his racing days he showed an affection for Shetland ponies as mascots. When he retired, he would not eat unless the little fellow alongside him ate, too. Exterminator wore out a Hapsburgian succession of Shetlands, for he lived to be thirty on Kilmer's green pastures. The stable help always praised him for being too polite to reveal he was aware that they were bringing him a new Shetland, but they said he knew when each of his companions died and that although he tried not to show it, he was distraught and grieved for days, all the while putting up a pretense of believing the new recruit was the same pony."

These ponies were all nicknamed Peanuts, and a story in a 1941 *Collier's* magazine told of the special relationship between Exterminator and one of his mascots.

"Peanuts is a Shetland pony who has been Exterminator's inseparable companion for sixteen years," the story said. "He and Old Bones still stage impromptu races, all of which follow a severe pattern laid down by Exterminator. Exterminator lets Peanuts take a lead, which pleases the old pony immensely. Then, with a mighty creaking of horse machinery, Old Bones breezes past Peanuts, and looks back triumphantly as of old.

"Old Bones kids Peanuts a lot, too. He'll nip at Peanuts' withers until the old pony is full of indignation and ready to kick him. Then, a split-second before the kick starts, Old Bones will lean down on Peanuts and Peanuts' hind hoofs will suddenly be pressed so hard down against the ground that he won't be able to get them up for the kick. Old Bones really loves Peanuts."

Later that same year, Exterminator paraded to the post at Pimlico before a race named in his honor. The old gelding, then twenty-six, was without a rider—but not without Peanuts—as he led the prerace parade.

The beloved Exterminator lived to the age of thirty, dying of a heart attack on September 26, 1945.

As far as Matt Winn was concerned, Exterminator was the best racehorse he ever saw.

"He could do everything," Winn said.

James Edward ("Sunny Jim") Fitzsimmons. (Courtesy New York Racing Association)

18

The Happiest Life

JAMES EDWARD ("SUNNY JIM") FITZSIMMONS *would* get around to taking his doctor's advice . . . just not in a hurry. Indeed, it took him more than three-quarters of a century.

In 1887, Fitzsimmons—a skinny exercise boy—was advised by a doctor to retire from racing and turn to the quiet life of a farmer. "Young man," the doctor told him, "you had better give up racing. Stay away from that excitement, or you won't last with that heart."

Fitzsimmons lasted with that heart, lasted until he finally decided in 1963 to call it quits. During his years on the turf, he became the only trainer of two Triple Crown champions (Gallant Fox in 1930 and Omaha in 1935). In addition, he trained two world-leading money-winning horses (Gallant Fox, $328,165, and Nashua, $1,288,565).

He trained for such famous names as the Belair Stud and the Wheatley Stable and had a barnful of the finest blue-blooded horseflesh in America. He did it all, and through many of those years he was known as "Sunny Jim," a fitting nickname for a man with such a twinkle in his eyes, a good nature, and an even disposition.

Mr. Fitz's genial personality was known to one and all.

Some cynics adopted a "this guy's too good to be true" attitude toward him and were determined to be hostile toward him when they were first introduced. But they were soon won over by Mr. Fitz's charm, ingenuousness, and warmth.

As busy as Mr. Fitz was on the racetrack, he always seemed to find a few moments for anybody—from the rich and famous to the newest groom in the stable.

Hard work paved the way for Mr. Fitz's success. "I like to sleep in the mornings," he would say. "If I had a way to beat them, I wouldn't be getting up at 4:30 every day."

Fitzsimmons was born July 23, 1874, in a little cottage on a farm in the village of Sheepshead Bay, N.Y. The house later was razed when the land on which it stood was purchased to build the Sheepshead Bay racetrack, which opened in 1880.

As a ten-year-old, Fitzsimmons began his career on the racetrack on March 4, 1885, the day Grover Cleveland was sworn in as president of the United States. He went to work as either a dishwasher in a track kitchen, errand boy, water boy, stable cook's helper, general helper, hot-walker or exercise rider for a stable—or a combination of any, or all, of the above. He slept in the loft.

In 1887, he contracted malaria at Long Branch, N.J., and suffered from palpitations of the heart. It was then the doctor advised him to give up racing and become a farmer. But young Fitzsimmons had some things he wanted to do before he settled down to a quiet life.

He rode his first race, at Brighton Beach, on August 7, 1889, aboard Newburg, owned by the Dwyer Brothers. More than a year later, he brought home his first winner—Crispin on September 13, 1890, at Gloucester City, N.J. Seventy-three years later, when he would retire, Mr. Fitz was asked to name his biggest thrill and he said it was this victory aboard Crispin in a one-mile race that carried a $250 purse. "We won, whipping, by 6 lengths," he would recall. He didn't give himself good grades for his performance aboard Crispin, later saying he came through with "a bad ride; the horse was a sixteenth of a mile in front in the stretch, and I started whipping him."

At the age of seventeen, he married Jennie Harvey, and together they raised six children (five sons and a daughter). Two of the sons, James J. and John, became chief assistants with the stable.

Fitzsimmons rode for about ten years, never distinguishing himself. He said he was "pretty mediocre" as a jockey. "I was vaccinated for jockey, but it didn't take," he declared.

He rode at the Guttenberg track "when they first held night racing under the lights," he recalled. "I hadn't had a winner in some time. When I got a chance to win one, I was halfway down the stretch when I saw something coming at me and I went to a drive. I needed that winner. When we pulled up, I found out we had won by 10 lengths. The other horse was my shadow chasing me. I knew enough to outride my shadow."

Mr. Fitz didn't live a pampered life as a jockey. "I once walked a horse fifteen miles to a racetrack, rode him in two heats and walked him back," he recalled. "The purse was five dollars, and I earned twenty-five cents."

Back in those days, there was a group of tracks in Pennsylvania, New Jersey, and Maspeth, N.Y., called "The Frying Pan Circuit," and that's where Fitzsimmons rode. Fitzsimmons, who never won a stakes race as a jockey, began to put on weight. He rode his last race in the 1901 Tidal Stakes at Sheepshead Bay, finishing fifth—and last—aboard Agnes D., a long shot whom he also trained at the time. It was Agnes D. who provided him with his first victory as a trainer—August 7, 1900 at Brighton Beach.

Before he began training, he was thinking about leaving the racetrack for a job as a streetcar motorman in Philadelphia. But a friend told him one morning to drop by a barn where he might land a job as a trainer. The job materialized, and thus began the training career of Sunny Jim Fitzsimmons.

When he started out on the leaky-roof circuit (minor tracks), he sometimes went without a meal to see that his horses were fed. From that beginning, he would go on to become America's most beloved horseman. He would win three runnings of the Kentucky Derby and a record thirteen Triple Crown races, he would make his way into racing's Hall of Fame, and, along the way, as "The Sage of Sheepshead Bay," he would gain the respect and admiration of all in racing.

Mr. Fitz trained for a variety of owners in his early years, people such as Sen. Johnson N. Camden of Kentucky and Ambassador Breckinridge Long. He also trained for Frank James of the "James Boys."

He began training for the Belair Stud of William Woodward, Sr., in 1923. His first stakes winner for Belair was Priscilla Ruley, a homebred who captured the 1924 Gazelle at Aqueduct.

Mr. Fitz became trainer for the Wheatley Stable of Mrs. Henry Carnegie Phipps and her brother, Ogden Mills, from its early beginning in the mid-1920s and developed the stable's first two stakes winners, Diavolo (one of his favorites) and Distraction. He later trained for Mrs. Phipps' son, Ogden, and for his son, Ogden Mills ("Dinny") Phipps. In the early 1960s, Mr. Fitz trained Dinny Phipps' first winner. Phipps, now chairman of The Jockey Club, recalled, "My first starter won, and all Mr. Fitz said after the race was: 'I did that also for your father and grandmother.'"

Fitzsimmons trained three Derby winners during the 1930s—Gallant Fox (1930), Omaha (1935), and Johnstown (1939). Other Derby horses trained by him during that decade included Granville, who won Horse of the Year fame in 1936 but unseated his jockey, Jimmy Stout, shortly after the start of the Derby that year, and Fighting Fox, a full brother to Gallant Fox (sixth in the 1938 renewal).

Of Gallant Fox, Fitzsimmons once said: "So long as he had competition he would run like the wind, but as soon as he whipped everybody and got the lead, he would slow to a walk. He was a fire-eater when he had the competition, though."

Fitzsimmons saw to it that Gallant Fox had the competition in his workouts. The crafty trainer was known to use a relay team of horses to work out with Gallant Fox. A sprint horse would start off with Gallant Fox and, at some point along the way during the workout, another would step in and pick up the action. Sometimes still another trial horse would come in as a replacement and hook Gallant Fox during the drill. All the better to keep Gallant Fox running hard throughout the workout.

Gallant Fox never won a race by more than 4 lengths and, all told, his eleven career triumphs were by a total of only 19½ to 21 lengths. But he still got the job done more times than not, and Mr. Fitz, who trained an honor roll of champions through the years, paid Gallant Fox a supreme compliment by calling him the best horse he ever had going a mile and a half. Distance races indeed were right down Gallant Fox's alley. He twice won at a mile and a half and triumphed in three even longer races—a mile and five-eighths, a mile and three-quarters, and two miles.

Asked his secret to success, Fitzsimmons was known to say, "Good horses and good bosses. A trainer needs a boss who will stick with him. Anybody who couldn't train for the people I work for just can't train."

In 1951, his wife died. Three years later, approaching his eightieth birthday, Fitzsimmons looked back and said, "I've been lucky. I've had good horses and good bosses, and I've had a job that keeps me out in the open air. I've met fine people and had good friends. It's been a good life."

At the age of eighty, most men wouldn't have much to look forward to, but that wasn't the case for Mr. Fitz, who still had a lot of living to do. In 1954, he was training Nashua, the best two-year-old colt in the land. Nashua was favored going into the 1955 Kentucky Derby, a race that Mr. Fitz didn't attend. "I don't ship so well anymore," he said, remaining in New York.

Mr. Fitz watched the Derby on television from the Belmont Park administration building, and he had no excuse following Swaps' 1½-length victory. "Swaps won that race all the way," Fitzsimmons said after the loss. "When Nashua challenged in the stretch, Swaps had more than enough left to beat him.

"Don't try to make me a bad loser," Mr. Fitz said. "Nashua is a fine horse. He was beaten by a great horse in a good race. There are more good races coming up, and we'll be in them, I'm sure."

Nashua went on from his loss in the Derby to win the Preakness and Belmont, races in which Swaps didn't run. Swaps wasn't nominated to either, and although he could have been supplemented to the Preakness, he wouldn't have been able to run in the Belmont, which didn't accept supplementary entries.

Those two future Hall of Famers met one other time in their career—the memorable match race of August 31, 1955 at Washington Park.

Before sending him to Chicago for this race, Fitzsimmons trained Nashua on Saratoga's deep, tiring track. "Training in Saratoga makes a horse fit," Fitzsimmons said. "In a match race, the object is to run from the gate, and the fittest horse wins."

Hall of Fame jockey Eddie Arcaro recalled riding Nashua against Swaps: "I just got beat on Nashua [in the Derby] by misjudging Swaps. I had seen Swaps out in California. He wasn't any kind of a horse, and I let him steal that lead on me—and, hell, when I went to him, he was a fresh horse when I got to him turnin' for home. I got up head-and-head with him. That's why in the match race I thought I'd beat him because I wasn't gonna let him get an inch away from me."

Nashua went to the lead at the outset of that match race and came home 6½ lengths on top of Swaps, who wasn't at his best that day. Afterward, Mr. Fitz said: "It was the greatest race we ever had in this country. It's my greatest race, too." Later, he would call this victory as his greatest thrill as a trainer.

The day after the match race, Greentree Stable co-owner

John Hay Whitney, who later would serve as U.S. ambassador to Great Britain from 1957 to 1961, was moved to quote his trainer, Princeton graduate John Gaver, in writing a letter to Fitzsimmons:

> Dear Mr. Fitz,
>
> John Gaver says, "That was the greatest victory since the Greeks beat somebody or other at Thermopylae or somewhere." And I know that his feeling comes from his great admiration and affection for you. Let me say how much I share these sentiments.
>
> You are truly a wizard in knowing what a horse can take, but more than that you bring great respect to racing. The public understands you, and you represent the finest traditions of this game we all love.
>
> With my admiration.
> Sincerely, John Hay Whitney.

Nashua, who earned the Horse of the Year title in 1955, set an American record of 3:20⅖ in winning the two-mile Jockey Club Gold Cup at Belmont Park on October 13, 1956. Five days later, at Keeneland Race Course in Kentucky, Nashua made his final public appearance before going off to stud at Spendthrift Farm. "He won his first and his last race and a lot in between, too," Fitzsimmons said. "He's my greatest horse."

At another time, Mr. Fitz said he ranked Nashua with Gallant Fox and Bold Ruler as the three best horses he ever trained. Near the end of his training career, he said, "It's hard to tell the best horse. I've had so many good ones that the only way I could pick out a best one would be to put the whole bunch of them together and race them."

Through the years, he trained four horses who were considered the best in America during their three-year-old seasons—Gallant Fox (1930), Granville (1936), Nashua (1955), and Bold Ruler (1957). All four ran in the Kentucky Derby; Gallant Fox was the only one to win the race.

Bold Ruler, Mr. Fitz's last Derby starter, ran in the greatest field in the race's history. Iron Liege won the '57 Derby by a nose over Gallant Man, with Round Table third and Bold Ruler fourth.

Arcaro rode Bold Ruler, who was favored at 6-5. "The only time Fitz ever gave me orders was on Bold Ruler in the Derby—the only time," Arcaro recalled. "And I made a mistake listening to him. He said, 'There's a lot of speed in this race. I think you ought to take him back.' I said, 'Mr. Fitz, he's won everything in front.' He said, 'Well, he'll come from behind.' But he was rank coming to that first turn. He was resenting it, and when he started resenting it, I should have just let him sneak off. But I was so close to Fitz, I would have felt awful if I had put him on the lead and then he had got beat. And he probably would have, by the way, because he wasn't a true mile-and-a-quarter horse."

In 1958, Mr. Fitz said that Bold Ruler probably could have defeated Gallant Fox and Nashua "up to a mile and an eighth."

But if Mr. Fitz had to bet on the outcome of a race featuring Bold Ruler, Gallant Fox, and Nashua, chances are he wouldn't have wagered more than a dollar or two. He simply didn't believe in betting a lot on the races.

"Dad liked to bet on horses but just plain hated to bet more than a dollar," his son John once recalled. "Dad was poison to any horse he bet on. We finally got him not to bet his dollars on our champions in big stakes, although sometimes he'd slip off from us and persuade some sucker he barely knew to split a bet with him on one of the big horses. Once he tried to get an old colored groom of ours to split a bet on Gallant Fox when he was odds-on. The groom said, 'Mr. Fitz, why would I bet a measly buck to win eighty cents? I got fifty dollars of my own money on The Fox already.' That made Dad furious. He didn't speak to the old man for weeks. He said it wasn't proper or decent for a guinea to bet fifty bucks on a horse when the trainer was only betting a dollar.

"When he couldn't get anybody else to split a bet with him, he'd come to me and say, 'Give me a dollar, John. We're splitting a bet on so-and-so.' Over the years, he dollared me to death, and we almost never won."

His grandson, James W. Fitzsimmons, recalled this story: "I heard John Gaver say one time, 'When you have an argument with Fitz, it just means you've lost another argument.' John Gaver was a well-educated man. So you can understand that the hired help didn't waste much time talking back to him. They just kept saying, 'Yes, sir.'

"He had this man called Charlie Brady who was his gofer—always with him. The old man never went into the stand, he never had a box, he never socialized. He'd go out into the centerfield or he'd go to the head of the stretch and watch his horses. If he saw an overlay, he would take a shot with $2. And there came this time where he and Charlie were walking out into the centerfield at Hialeah—and, for whatever reason, he looked up and he saw the odds board and he said, 'Charlie, this horse shouldn't be that price. Go get me a $2 ticket.' And Charlie went running and got the $2 ticket and came back out into the centerfield. And then the race was off, and the horse won by 5 with the jock standing up. And the old man said to Charlie, 'Charlie, I told you that horse shouldn't be 15 to 1.' And Charlie said, 'Mr. Fitz, that horse was 1 to 5.' The old man didn't see the red spot between 1 and 5—for whatever reason, it was blocked—and Charlie went and collected the $2.40 for him."

It seems Mr. Fitz's frugal betting habits came about after losing a sizable wager on Man o' War in the 1919 Sanford Memorial. Man o' War lost the Sanford, the only blemish in his twenty-one-race career. "He never carried much money in his pockets, so he hustled around and borrowed five here and ten there and twenty some other place until he had a hundred," said John Fitzsimmons.

"Man o' War taught me a lesson," Mr. Fitz said. "He proved that there's never a sure thing. Only once in his career was he ever beaten. But that was the time I made my first $100 bet—and my last."

Late in life, he said, "I bet only for pure devilment. Betting on horses to make money is downright foolishness. But devilment's all right."

Fitzsimmons saddled horses throughout the country, but

the New York tracks were his favorite. "When you're away from New York," he said, "you're camping out."

When he retired in 1963, he had ranked as the leading money-winning trainer five times (1930, 1932, 1936, 1939, and 1955). Records aren't complete for the early part of his career, but it is known that he saddled the winners of 2,275 races. He trained 149 stakes winners, some of whom triumphed repeatedly in added-money races.

It was in 1963, the year of Mr. Fitz's retirement, that Red Smith wrote: "Every August for some years now, one Sunday has been given over to a party at Fitzsimmonsville, the cottage colony on Lake Desolation where Mr. Fitz and his remarkable tribe live during the Saratoga meeting. The first time it was proposed, Mr. Fitz took a dim view. 'A party?' he said. 'Who'd ever want to come?' Outnumbered and overruled, he gave reluctant consent, but as the day approached he fretted and stewed, nervous as a bride. Chances are nobody knows whether there were 100 guests or 250, for who was counting? But it was a howling success, as it had to be, and Mr. Fitz was delighted. 'Kathie,' he told his granddaughter—he was only about eighty then, 'Kathie, if the good Lord spares you, we'll do it again.' The good Lord has, and they have."

Whitney Tower, a former distinguished member of the *Sports Illustrated* and *Classic* magazine staffs, also wrote of Mr. Fitz and Saratoga: "Hardly more than a furlong away from Saratoga's National Museum of Racing, Mr. Fitz would hold daily court in the Saratoga track paddock. He sat, each August afternoon, on the same bench under the same elms and one needed no appointment to sign up for a bit of learning. 'Son,' he would say to anyone within earshot, 'the owners of racehorses are the greatest people on earth. They pay the bills with little chance of making any money.'"

Racing is a sport that can keep people humble, and nobody was any humbler than Mr. Fitz. "Nobody can make a bad horse good," he said. "The main object is to avoid making a good horse bad, and a lot of it is just a matter of luck. I came into this game with nothing to give it. Racing gave me the happiest life you could want. Racing doesn't owe me a thing, but I owe the game a hell of a lot."

He also had this bit of philosophy: "Horses are like people. They're brave or cowardly, gentle or mean, willing or stubborn. Sometimes they're like children. That's when you should love 'em a lot, but don't let 'em get away with anything."

Sunny Jim Fitzsimmons in later life. (Courtesy New York Racing Association)

In his later years, he was forced to stoop over almost double because of a spinal arthritic condition, but he still rose at dawn each day to train his horses. Resting on two canes, he would slowly go about his training duties in the mornings. He wouldn't watch the races, however, preferring to remain in a quiet spot in the paddock or barn area while his horses were running.

He always remained upbeat, his sprightly nature never wavering. "The older you get," he once said, "the more you realize that life itself is a game of luck. The big thing is to wind up with people still liking you. If you can do that, you're a pretty lucky guy."

In April 1963, Mr. Fitz announced that he would retire after seventy-eight years in racing. "I just can't get around as well as I used to—that's all," he said. "These people have a big investment in their stock, and it must be protected. I know I can't do the things I should be doing, and I thought about retiring a few months ago."

On his final day, June 15, 1963, it was business as usual for the eighty-eight-year-old trainer. He arrived at Belmont Park at 6:00 A.M., putting in a full morning's work before he headed to Aqueduct. In a sentimental farewell ceremony that old-timers still recall, the stooped-over trainer raised his hat to the cheers of the 48,160 fans at Aqueduct. Mrs. Phipps presented him with a silver tray engraved with the names of the stakes horses he had trained.

In 1965, Mr. Fitz said: "I can remember things that happened to me since I was four and five years old. Of course, I do have trouble remembering the names of my great-grandchildren, but then I have forty-one. I'm the happiest guy in the world. I'm so lucky to be in such good health at ninety. I feel sorry for people with aches and pains. When I get an ache, sometimes I feel sorry for myself. I feel well enough now to still be training horses, but I can't get around. A trainer has to know how every one of his horses sleeps and eats and trains. He can't take someone else's word for it."

This Grand Old Man of Racing died on March 11, 1966.

The eighty-eight-year-old Mr. Fitz waved good-bye to the crowd on June 15, 1963. (Courtesy New York Racing Association)

He was ninety-one years old. *The New York Times* started his obituary on the first page—not the first page of the sports section, but the first page of the newspaper.

"His heart just gave out," said John Fitzsimmons, his white-haired son.

It was a heart that lasted a long time—much longer than a doctor back in 1887 ever dreamed it would.